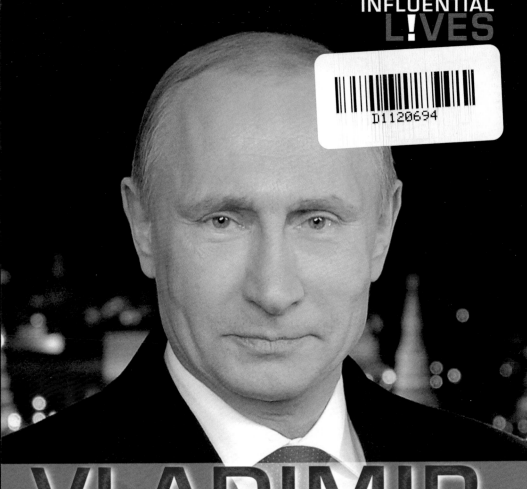

D1120694

VLADIMIR PUTIN

RUSSIAN PRIME MINISTER AND PRESIDENT

Susan Nichols

Enslow Publishing
101 W. 23rd Street
Suite 240
New York, NY 10011
USA
enslow.com

Published in 2019 by Enslow Publishing, LLC.
101 W. 23rd Street, Suite 240, New York, NY 10011

Library of Congress Cataloging-in-Publication Data
Names: Nichols, Susan, 1975- author.
Title: Vladimir Putin / Susan Nichols.
Description: New York : Enslow Publishing, 2019. | Series: Influential lives
| Includes bibliographical references and index. | Audience: Grade 7 to 12.
Identifiers: LCCN 2017018163 | ISBN 9780766092044 (library bound) | 9781978501737 (paperback)
Subjects: LCSH: Putin, Vladimir Vladimirovich, 1952– | Presidents—Russia
(Federation)—Biography. | Russia (Federation)—Politics and
government—1991-
Classification: LCC DK510.766.P87 N53 2017 | DDC 947.086092 [B] —dc23
LC record available at https://lccn.loc.gov/2017018163

Printed in the United States of America

To Our Readers: We have done our best to make sure all websites in this book were active and appropriate when we went to press. However, the author and the publisher have no control over and assume no liability for the material available on those websites or on any websites they may link to. Any comments or suggestions can be sent by e-mail to customerservice@enslow.com.

Photo credits: Cover, p. 1 Alexey Druzhinin/AFP/Getty Images; p. 4 Mikhail Metzel/TASS/Getty Images; p. 11 Fox Photos/Hulton Archive/Getty Images; pp. 13, 46, 53, 63 SVF2/Universal Images Group/Getty Images; pp. 14, 18, 39 Laski Diffusion/Hulton Archive/Getty Images; pp. 23, 75 © AP Images; p. 26 Robert Wallis/Corbis Historical/Getty Images; p. 29 Mario De Biasi/Mondadori Portfolio/Getty Images; p. 32 The White House/Hulton Archive/Getty Images; p. 44 Vittoriano Rastelli/Corbis Historical/Getty Images; p. 49 Oleg Nikishin/AFP/Getty Images; p. 58 Stringer/ AFP/Getty Images; p. 66 Dirck Halstead/Hulton Archive/Getty Images; p. 69 Scott Peterson/ Getty Images; p. 77 Oleg Nikishin/Getty Images; p. 81 Markus Leodolter/AFP/Getty Images; p. 84 Mikhail Klimentyev/AFP/Getty Images; p. 90 Alexey Nikolsky/AFP/Getty Images; p. 95 Sipa USA/ AP Images; p. 102 Hannah Peters/Getty Images; back cover and interior pages background graphic zffoto/Shutterstock .com.

Contents

Introduction

In 2016, the United States of America experienced one of its most controversial presidential elections. The two main contenders—Democratic candidate Hillary Clinton and Republican candidate Donald Trump—were both fairly unpopular among American voters. In fact, at the end of the summer, *USAToday* announced, "Among U.S. adults, Clinton now has a 56% unfavorability rating, while Trump had 63%,"[1] which means that more people *disliked* the candidates than liked them. It seemed that the next president would be elected for being the "lesser of two evils."

To have two unpopular candidates was an unusual situation for American voters. Clinton was plagued by a series of scandals, including questions about whether she'd accepted donations to her family foundation from

Although seen by much of the world as an authoritarian leader, Russian president Vladimir Putin is very popular among his country's citizens.

5

people who wanted to influence her when she was serving as secretary of state. Another scandal included whether, as secretary of state, she had used a personal email server to communicate. The problem, if it were true, was that a personal server would make her more susceptible to being hacked by foreign powers. The Clinton email scandal reminded Americans of the fact that one of the new ways foreign powers conducted warfare was cyberwarfare, which means that one country will spy on or hack into another nation's electronic communications and records to cull information that will help it. How real is cyberwarfare? It's very real and very serious.

In fact, it was revealed during the election that the Democratic National Committee (DNC) *had* been hacked. As Republicans rejoiced at the opposition party's bad fortune, something more serious was uncovered. The hack was traced to operatives in a country that had been an enemy of the United States for years: Russia, led by President Vladimir Putin.

The hack of the DNC records by the Russians was so serious that it was described like this by the *New York Times*:

> Imagine the headlines if, in 2015, Russian agents had leapt out of a van at 2 a.m. in Southeast Washington and broken into the Democratic National Committee offices using sophisticated tools and techniques to steal tens of thousands of documents, including the names and Social Security numbers of donors and employees, and confidential memorandums about campaign strategy for the presidential election.[2]

There was agreement among US national security and intelligence agencies that Vladimir Putin had not only had knowledge of but had approved this hack. According to NBC news, "U.S. intelligence officials now believe with 'a high level of confidence' that Russian President Vladimir Putin became personally involved in the covert Russian campaign to interfere in the U.S. presidential election [. . .] Putin personally directed how hacked material from Democrats was leaked and otherwise used."[3]

The Russian interference didn't stop there. Since the election victory of Donald Trump, his presidency has been tainted by connections to Russians, particularly Vladimir Putin. Trump's national security advisor, Michael Flynn, had to resign after serving only twenty-four days when it was revealed that he had been in close contact with representatives of Russia. Furthermore, when the US government decided to investigate Russian interference in the US elections, newly sworn-in attorney general Jeff Sessions had to recuse himself from the investigation. Why? Because he admitted that he had met with the Russian ambassador during the election, while he was campaigning for his close friend Donald Trump.

Months later, in May 2017, a similar incident occurred in France ahead of that country's presidential election. Emails of liberal candidate Emmanuel Macron were hacked and released just days before voters went to the booths to decide between Macron and far-right candidate Marine LePen. Suspicion was immediately directed at Russia, due to the similarities to the US hack and also to Putin's connections to LePen, but there is so far no conclusive evidence that Putin or his associates were responsible for the hack, which seemed to have little effect on the outcome. Still, with many pending elections throughout Europe in the near future, the world waited to see if interference would be a common theme.

Who is Vladimir Putin, and how has he managed to cause such a furor over the US and other western nations' elections? This resource will detail his early years and rise in Russia, as well as his growing role in international politics.

CHAPTER ONE

A Challenging Childhood

· · · · · · · · · · · · · · ·

Vladimir Vladimirovich Putin was born on October 7, 1952, in a time when his nation was experiencing many changes and the average citizen endured a difficult life. In fact, Putin's early years were quite challenging.

His father was Vladimir Spiridonovich Putin, and his mother was Maria Ivanovna Shelomova. The elder Putin and Shelomova met each other during the turbulent years of World War I, which lasted from 1914 to 1918. According to Putin himself, his father's family had lived in St. Petersburg during the war, but when things became too dire, they moved to Pominovo, his grandmother's village. He has said, "It was in Pominovo that my father met my mother, and they got married at the age of 17."[1]

The couple moved back to St. Petersburg after the war. There, in Russia's second most populated city, they started their lives together.

However, many changes occurred in Russia during and after World War I. One of them was the city of St. Petersburg itself, whose name had been changed to Petrograd. Germany had been Russia's enemy during the war, so anti-German sentiments were running high. For many people who were still traumatized by the war, the name "St. Petersburg" sounded too German. "Petrograd" was more Russian—and more patriotic.

Petrograd would undergo many more name changes. By the time Vladimir Putin was born, it would be renamed Leningrad, and later, when the Soviet Union eventually collapsed, it would revert to St. Petersburg.

The USSR

Before Putin was born, Russia had been an empire, led by Czar Nicholas II, who was overthrown in March 1917 by Russians frustrated with imperial rule. The czar's government had been corrupt, and Russia's involvement in World War I had been disastrous for its people.

The provisional government that was formed to usher in a peaceful transition was itself overthrown a short while later during the Bolshevik Revolution in October 1917. The Bolsheviks were a political party led by Vladimir Lenin, and they promoted a Marxist government. Their ideas differed from those of Karl Marx, who originated the theory, but essentially, they opposed capitalism and wanted to establish government control over the economy. Under Lenin, Russia became a communist nation. Czar Nicholas was executed by the Bolsheviks on July 17, 1918, and Russia, under Lenin,

Communist Party leader Joseph Stalin (1879–1953) dominated Soviet politics for decades. Though he helped the Soviet Union defeat the Nazis during World War II, he ruled through brute force.

became known as the Russian Soviet Federative Socialist Republic, or the Russian SFSR.

The SFSR was not to last long, however, as the Russians consolidated power. In 1922, the Union of Soviet Socialist Republics (USSR) was established, with Lenin as its head. Lenin died in 1924, which ushered in the leadership of Joseph Stalin, who was essentially a dictator. He has become known as one of the most brutal leaders in world history for his suppression of oppositional ideas.

It was under Stalin that the USSR became embroiled in World War II (1939–1945), during which the Russians—

Stalin: Soviet Dictator

One of the most famous leaders in world history was Joseph Stalin, the feared dictator of the Union of Soviet Socialist Republics (USSR). Stalin was born in 1878. His family was very poor, and he became involved in criminal and political activities. He joined the Communists. When Vladimir Lenin died, there were several people vying for power. Among these, Stalin rose to the top, and he assumed power in 1929. Under Stalin's rule, the USSR transformed from a peasant, rural society into an industrialized and modern world power. However, the Stalin regime used brutal tactics to suppress criticism and opposition, and it was common for people who questioned Stalin or challenged his authority to be executed. Millions of people died during his rule.

During World War II, Nazis attacked Leningrad. The Siege of Leningrad lasted almost nine hundred days. This photo depicts Mayakovsky Street, in Leningrad, during a Nazi attack in September 1942.

• • • • • • • • • • • • • • • • • • • •

allied with the United States, the United Kingdom, and other nations—sought to suppress the violent Nazi regime of Adolf Hitler and his allies.

The city of Leningrad (the former St. Petersburg) endured one of the most terrible events during World War II. Many historians believe that it is important to understand Leningrad's tragic history to understand the personality and character of Vladimir Putin.

In the summer of 1941, Nazi forces had surrounded the city of Leningrad and cut off all supplies to its citizens. The people of Leningrad suffered greatly. The Soviet Red Army wasn't able to drive off the Germans until 1943. In total, Leningrad was under siege for nine hundred days, and one million inhabitants died.

During the Siege of Leningrad, Putin's father, Vladimir, joined the special forces to stave off the German assault. He often fought behind German lines, and one day, he suffered an injury while fighting. The injury was quite bad, and Vladimir performed other tasks to provide for his family. During this time, his mother, who was also working hard, nearly starved to death.

Vladimir Putin is pictured with his parents, Maria and Vladimir. Putin has written and spoken admiringly of his parents, who suffered greatly, as many Russians did, during the war.

The *Atlantic* writer Joseph Burgo emphasizes the fact that Putin was born eight years after the siege. The event had a profound impact on his upbringing. "Vladimir was born into this atmosphere of hunger, disability, and profound grief." Burgo continues, "The city bore physical and emotional scars for decades afterward," and Putin's parents had survived but suffered greatly, both physically (as a result of the siege) and personally. The Putins had already lost two sons, older than Vladimir. One son had died as an infant before World War II, and the other had died shortly after the war ended.[2]

By the time Vladimir was born, his parents were in their early forties and the war had left them poor, like other residents of the city. They lived in a communal, overcrowded building, known as a *kommunalka* in Russian.

"I never discuss issues related to my family."[3]

It was an old building, with a deteriorating structure. According to Putin, "I come from an ordinary family, and this is how I lived for a long time, nearly my whole life. I lived as an average, normal person and I have always maintained that connection."[4]

Putin's father worked in a factory, and his mother also worked in any job that was available, which left their young child unattended for long periods of time. He spent his childhood hanging out with the people in the building, many of whom were not positive influences.

According to Burgo, there were several other children around him who were troublemakers and miscreants.

Because he spent time with them, their influence rubbed off on young Vladimir. "Though younger and smaller than many of them," Burgo writes, "Putin fought back against the courtyard thugs and became something of a bully himself."[5] He began to see that being strong and showing that one was willing to fight was a valuable asset, at least in his specific environment.

Badly Behaved in School

Vladimir enrolled in school in 1960, attending the local Leningrad primary school. After the eighth grade, he entered a magnet high school with an emphasis on chemistry and technology, and he graduated in 1970. He did not always behave well in school, although his teachers could see that he was intelligent.

His fifth-grade teacher, Vera Gurevich, said, "In the fifth grade, he still hadn't found himself yet, but I could feel the potential, the energy and the character in him. I saw that he had a great deal of interest in language; he picked it up easily. He had a very good memory and an agile mind. I thought, something good will come of this boy, so I decided to give him more attention, to distract him from the boys on the streets."[6]

Not all his teachers felt this way about young Vladimir. Recently, the popular Russian tabloid paper *Komsomolskaya Pravda* published an article after discovering Putin's gradebook from his school days. The gradebook had been found in "the dusty attic of a small wooden house where he spent his childhood summers," in the town of Tosno, near Leningrad.[7] The grades and comments from his teachers offer a picture of a student who behaved badly.

His grades were quite average, which might surprise people who assumed he was academically very strong in school. According to ABC News, "On the Soviet five-point scale, he scored threes in arithmetic and natural science, and a two in drawing. The only subject in which he scored a five was history."[9]

> **"I was always late for my first class, so even in winter I didn't have time to dress properly."**[8]

One of his teacher's commented, "Before class [Putin] threw chalkboard erasers at the children." Another wrote, "Didn't do his math homework." Other comments included, "Behaved badly during singing class" and "Talks in class."[10] He often forgot school items, such as his uniform, and he was caught passing notes to other boys in class.

A New Focus

Vera Gurevich implored Vladimir to focus more on his grades, even reaching out to his father to influence him. Putin recalls that, in sixth grade, he began to understand that his schoolwork mattered and that he should pay attention to his grades. According to his official government website, he says, "It became clear that street smarts were not enough, so I began doing sports. But even that was not enough for maintaining my status, so

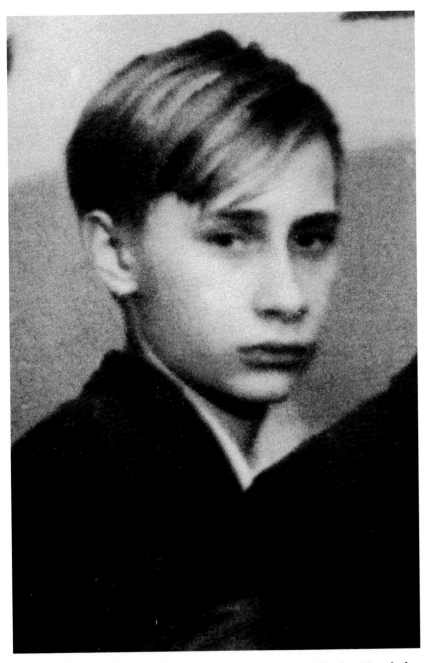

This 1966 class photo of Vladimir Putin was taken while he attended grade school. By all accounts, he was not a high academic achiever, but he became more serious about his studies as he got older.

to speak, for very long. I realised that I also needed to study well."[11]

He had been interested in sports, especially in the martial arts. At the age of eleven, he began training in judo, a form of martial arts that emerged from Japan in the late 1800s. A combat sport that derived from jujitsu, judo emphasizes discipline of body and mind and works by unbalancing one's opponent.

Putin's first judo trainer was Anatoly Rakhlin, who would become a lifelong friend. Later in his life, Putin reflected on how deeply judo had influenced him: "Judo teaches self-control," he said, "the ability to feel the moment, to see the opponent's strengths and weaknesses,

The Birth of Judo

Japan was ruled for centuries by professional soldiers, the samurai, who perfected martial arts. In their training, they used hand-to-hand combat, which they could use to attack and/or defend themselves. Jigoro Kano was born into a wealthy Japanese family in 1860. Due to his poor health and small physique, he started learning jujitsu, one of the martial arts, for self-defense. However, he became so immersed in the skills he learned that he opened his own school at the age of twenty-one, teaching a new form of martial arts that combined several styles of jujitsu. This new form was a gentler way because it also combined mental and moral discipline along with physical skill. It was called judo, which means "the gentle way."

to strive for the best result." He added that these were "essential abilities and skills for any politician."[12]

After high school, Putin enrolled at Leningrad State University, where he studied law. He earned his degree in 1975. In college, his mentor was Anatoly Aleksandrovich Sobchak, a legal scholar and a graduate of the state university himself. Sobchak was critical of the government, which made him popular among his students. Later, Sobchak would be instrumental in helping Putin launch his own political career.

Putin also became interested in governmental intelligence, which refers to information collected for the purpose of the security of one's nation. Intelligence can take the form of communications between government leaders, images or pictures taken of people and activities, and information gathered from one's network of informants, among other things. Every government has an intelligence bureau that analyzes information it has gathered and uses it to make decisions that keep the nation safe.

In 1975, after graduating from Leningrad State University, Putin joined the Komitet Gosudarstvennoy Bezopasnosti, known as the KGB, the USSR's security bureau. Specifically, he enlisted in its Foreign Intelligence Service.

Some research indicates that the law department at the state university was a way for the government to actually mentor and encourage talented students to enlist in the KGB. The KGB was established in 1954, after Joseph Stalin's death. According to journalist Reiss Smith, "Its mission was to serve as the 'sword and shield' of the dictatorial Communist Party."[13] It earned the reputation for being an effective and often brutal secret police force that spied on citizens and foreigners alike. Smith adds that the KGB, at one point, was the world's largest spy network, with "over 480,000 personnel at its height—many of them foreign nationals working undercover—and millions of informers."[14]

Putin became one of these officers. He seems to have been anticipating his work for the KGB. A *Washington Post* article reports that Putin said, about joining the force, "You know, I even wanted it. . . I was driven by high motives. I thought I would be able to use my skills to the best for society."[15]

Putin had dreamed of being in the KGB for years. According to Chris Bowlby, "Putin had wanted to join the KGB since he was a teenager, inspired by popular Soviet stories of secret service bravado in which, he recalled later, 'One man's effort could achieve what whole armies could not. One spy could decide the fate of thousands of people.'"[16]

CHAPTER TWO

Personal Life

I n 1983, Putin married Lyudmila Aleksandrovna Shkrebneva, who was working as a flight attendant for a Russian airline. They met at a ballet performance, a meeting that seems to have been arranged by a mutual friend. Lyudmila had attended Leningrad State University, where she studied foreign languages.

On his website, Putin states, "I knew that if I did not marry for another two or three years, I would not marry at all. True, I was used to life as a bachelor, but Lyudmila changed that."[1]

The couple married in 1983, and their first child, Maria, was born in 1985. A second daughter, Katerina (known as Katja), was born in 1986 in East Germany. According to Putin's website, "Both girls were named in honour of their grandmothers, Maria Putina and Yekaterina Shkrebneva."[2]

Putin had been assigned to work in East Germany, which was under communist control, in 1985. Putin

Putin married flight attendant Lyudmila Aleksandrovna Shkrebneva in 1983, and they went on to raise two daughters. The couple would divorce three decades later.

• •

speaks German fluently, and most newspaper reports and biographies agree that Putin was working as a spy for the KGB during this time period. The specifics of what he did are unknown, but one story stands out as being an influential moment on the young officer.

In 1989, the Berlin Wall was torn down by protestors who wanted to unite East and West Germany. One day,

> **"[My daughters] live in Russia ... They have never been educated anywhere except Russia. I am proud of them, they continue to study and are working."**[3]

after the fall, protestors decided to march on the KGB headquarters in Dresden. Putin came out and warned the crowd that the Soviet officers were armed and would use their weapons if they needed to. The protestors disbanded, but Putin called the leadership of a locally stationed Soviet army tank unit. He requested protection for KGB headquarters in case the protestors returned. The unit's leader told him that they could take orders only from Moscow, and "Moscow is silent."[4] Putin was apparently stunned by how the Soviet leadership was paralyzed to act because of public demonstrations and civil protests. It ran against his belief in a strong military and a strong government that Moscow should back down now.

In 1990, Putin's work for the KGB in East Germany ended, and the family returned to the Soviet Union. Lyudmila became a professor of German at Leningrad State University, while the two girls attended a German school in Moscow. Putin himself was assigned the position of assistant to the rector at the university, where he was in charge of international affairs.

Lyudmila and Vladimir Putin worked hard to maintain their privacy and especially the privacy of their daughters. In an NBC news report, Hasani Gittens writes, "The Putin girls may be the most mysterious first-children in modern history—especially when you

East Germany

One of the Eastern Bloc countries, East Germany was created after World War II. At the Yalta Conference, the Allied powers (the United States, the Soviet Union, and the United Kingdom) divided the defeated Nazi German state into zones. The Western Allies, such as the United States, controlled West Germany, while the Soviets controlled East Germany, which became Communist and repressive. Berlin, Germany's capital city, was also divided, and a wall was built in 1961 to prevent East Germans from crossing over into West Germany. That wall finally came down in 1989, and Germany was reunified in 1990, the year that Putin returned to the Soviet Union.

consider their father has held power, either as Prime Minister or as President, for nearly two decades."[5] They were rarely allowed to be photographed, for example, and the Putins did not speak about them in public. Both Maria and Katja went to the same university their parents attended, which was later renamed St. Petersburg State University. Maria studied biology, while Katja focused on Asian studies.

Even later, when he was Russia's leader, Putin hardly ever mentioned his daughters. The *New York Post* reported once that, in 2015, he did indulge in some bragging about his daughters' achievements. In a press conference, Putin said, "[Maria and Katja] studied only at

In November 1989, Germans destroyed the Berlin Wall, which had separated democratic West Germany and Communist East Germany. Soon, the two Germanys were rejoined as one nation.

• •

Russian universities. I am proud of them. They continue to study and work. My daughters speak three European languages fluently. One of them can even speak one or two Oriental languages. They are making their first steps and are successful."[6]

What is known about them is that Katja is athletic and spent time as an acrobatic dancer for several years. In 2016, she made a rare appearance in a dance competition, where her performance with her dance partner was filmed. (The Putin daughters have rarely been seen in photographs or film.) She married Russian billionaire Kirill Shamalov, and she owns a construction company in Russia. Her older

> **"They have never been 'star' children, they have never got pleasure from the spotlight being aimed at them. They just live their own lives."**[7]

sister, Maria, eventually earned a medical degree and is married to a Dutch businessman, but she lives in Moscow, where she reportedly has a daughter.

Soviet Politics

Putin became involved in local politics at the time that his family returned to the Soviet Union in 1990. On August 20, 1991, he formally resigned from his position with the KGB, having earned the rank of lieutenant colonel.

While working at Leningrad State University, he hoped to continue his studies and earn a PhD. However, he quickly became immersed in politics.

During this time, the Soviet Union was led by the Communist Party, which was the sole governing party in the nation. The Communist Party had been established in 1912 and seized power in 1917, after the Bolshevik Revolution. By the mid-1980s, the USSR had a strong economy, but the Communist Party's corruption was evident.

When it was formed, the Communist Party had been dedicated to the concept of democratic centralism.

The idea was created by Vladimir Lenin, who wanted to combine the open discussion and debate that was important in a democracy with the practical discipline of centralized party control. Therefore, in democratic centralism, the nation was ruled by a vanguard party, the Communists, who maintained control and a tight organizational structure; however, within their party, they tolerated open debate as a way of airing useful ideas and critiques.

As Lenin envisioned it, democratic centralism was a perfect system. Discussion was not permitted to go on without an end; in order to curtail internal trouble, at some point, the debate would stop, a vote would be held, and all party members would abide by that decision.

Despite this ideal, leaders such as Joseph Stalin had clamped down on much of the "democracy" in democratic centralism. The Communist Party assumed more and more governing power until it became a monopoly. By the mid-1980s, the Communist Party ran all aspects of the government—national and local—in the Soviet Union.

The structure of the Communist Party was rigid and hierarchical. There was a party Congress, which was led by a Central Committee. The Central Committee consisted of approximately three hundred members, and it elected members to other, smaller committees. Two of these committees were the most powerful ones in the entire Soviet Union. The Secretariat was the committee that oversaw the government's regular administrative work, while the politburo—which consisted of only twenty-four members—was the supreme authority in the nation, responsible for all domestic and foreign policy.

This structure allowed for the rise of dictators, like Stalin. The general secretary of the Central Committee was inarguably the most powerful person in the Soviet Union. Over the years, as one dictator after the next dominated the Soviet government, the ideals Lenin had once hoped for were diminished. Members of the Communist Party focused on making themselves

While many Communist leaders in the Soviet Union lived lavish lifestyles, average citizens suffered. People often stood in line for hours or even days to get staples such as bread and medicine.

wealthier, while the people—whose welfare they were supposed to champion—languished in poverty and were silenced by a brutal police force.

According to the *New York Times*, the Communist Party "created an unspeakably bleak society—polluted, chronically short of everything, stripped of initiative and spirituality."[8] While the average Soviet citizen suffered, standing in line for rations, Communist leaders lived lavishly: "grandiose candelabras, massive cars, vast hunting estates, armies of sycophants, secret hospitals filled with the latest Western technology."[9]

By the mid-1980s, many people within the Communist Party sought to reform the government. One of those reformers, Mikhail Gorbachev, became the general secretary of the Central Committee of the Communist Party in 1985. While Putin was still serving in the KGB's office in East Germany, Gorbachev was advocating two major changes in the USSR: *perestroika* and *glasnost*.

Perestroika was a restructuring of the Soviet government that Gorbachev proposed almost immediately. While the Soviet economy was strong, the lives of its individual citizens was, on average, poor. He believed that this was because economic decisions were largely in the hands of a small number of people in the Communist Party. Perestroika took away some of that power. "It also focused on economic issues, replacing the centralized government planning that had been a hallmark of the Soviet system with a greater reliance on market forces," explains an article on History.com.[10] In other words, economic decisions would be based on the natural shifts and trends in the market, which is closer to capitalism than communism.

Years later, when the Soviet Union had fallen apart, upon leaving office, Gorbachev reflected on his initiative and why he'd felt it was so vital to implement radical change:

> We had a lot of everything—land, oil and gas, other natural resources—and there was intellect and talent in abundance. However, we were living much worse than people in the industrialized countries were living and we were increasingly lagging behind them. The reason was obvious even then. This country was suffocating in the shackles of the bureaucratic command system. Doomed to cater to ideology, and suffer and carry the onerous burden of the arms race, it found itself at the breaking point.
>
> All the half-hearted reforms—and there have been a lot of them—fell through, one after another. This country was going nowhere and we couldn't possibly live the way we did. We had to change everything radically.[11]

Gorbachev also implemented glasnost, which means "openness." He wanted the Soviet Union to become more democratic, rather than centralized. He discontinued close Communist Party control over the newspapers and other media, and he allowed people and organizations to speak more freely than they had been permitted to do in decades. "By 1988, Gorbachev had expanded his reforms to include democratization, moving the USSR toward an elected form of government."[12] In other words, as the economy opened up to market forces, the general public and the Soviet media had an opportunity to comment

Soviet president Mikhail Gorbachev (*left*) pursued improved relations with former enemy the United States. In this December 1987 photo, he poses with US president Ronald Reagan in the White House during a visit to the United States.

on and critique the government's actions without fear of reprisal.

Gorbachev also pursued a closer relationship with the Soviet Union's biggest rival: the United States. He met with American president Ronald Reagan between 1985 and 1988, and both men signed an agreement to commit to reducing their individual nation's nuclear arms stockpiles. After years of having been engaged in a cold war with the United States, it seemed that the Soviets were on the path to a more productive relationship.

Finally, Gorbachev tried to lessen the political domination of the Soviet Union over other nations.

The Cold War

The cold war refers to a decades-long era in which the Soviet Union and the United States of America were locked in political tension. The United States disliked the Soviet Communist system and resisted its attempts to spread Communism to Asia and other parts of the globe. The Soviets felt that the United States had an aggressive position of intervening in international affairs and resented its growing power. The two nations fought proxy wars in other countries (including the Korean War and the Vietnam War), rather than confront each other directly; both nations possessed nuclear weapons and feared a direct conflict would be devastating.

There were a group of European countries that sat on the western border of the Soviet Union's biggest country, Russia. Known as the Eastern Bloc, these countries—including Bulgaria, Albania, Czechoslovakia, Hungary, East Germany, Poland, Romania, and Yugoslavia—were tied in an alliance with the Soviets by military force. For example, in Germany, an actual wall had been built in Berlin to separate West Germany, which was capitalist, from East Germany, which fell under Soviet Communist control.

In a 1988 speech to the United Nations, Gorbachev announced a major reduction of Soviet forces in the Eastern Bloc countries:

> By agreement with our Warsaw Treaty allies, we have decided to withdraw by 1991 six tank divisions from East Germany, Czechoslovakia and Hungary, and to disband them. Assault landing troops and several other formations and units, including assault crossing units with their weapons and combat equipment, will also be withdrawn from the groups of Soviet forces stationed in those countries. Soviet forces stationed in those countries will be reduced by 50,000 men and their armaments, by 5,000 tanks.[13]

He also stated that these nations would be free to decide whether or not they wanted to remain allied with the Soviet Union.

The news was welcomed by many around the world as a great thawing of rigid Soviet control over these countries, many of which had wished to be free of communism for years. However, within the Soviet Union, many who were loyal to the idea of the

Soviet Union worried that this was the end of their influence. Were the days of a strong Soviet Union coming to an end?

It was during this hectic time in Putin's life, when his political career was rising, that the Soviet Union's power began to fade.

CHAPTER THREE

The Soviet Union in Crisis

· · · · · · · · · · · · ·

On Christmas Day 1991, the Soviet Union officially came to an end. Gorbachev made a speech on that day, and shortly after he concluded it, the Soviet flag—bearing the symbols of the sickle and hammer—was lowered from the Kremlin, and the flag of the Russian Federation was raised.

It was a stunning end to a union that had been a world superpower, the greatest rival of the United States. What had brought about such a shocking dissolution? Gorbachev's policies of perestroika and glasnost had been implemented too quickly, and the results he'd hoped for—a revival of the Soviet economy—had not happened as rapidly as anticipated. People were out of work, lines formed at food centers, and companies and industries were going bankrupt. According to the *Guardian*, "The final years of the USSR are plagued by empty grocery stores, queues for food and widespread shortages."[1]

Furthermore, inspired by Gorbachev's openness, many Soviet allies began to break away from the Soviet Union and to reject Communism. Emboldened by their new ability to hold public demonstrations and to openly oppose

> **"Russia—we—are constantly being taught about democracy. But for some reason those who teach us do not want to learn themselves."[2]**

Communist policies, Czechoslovakia, Azerbaijan, Ukraine, Lithuania, and other countries all began to demand independence and the right to form their own governments, free from Soviet influence. There was a tremendous fear among Soviet loyalists that many of these countries would soon secede, which would devastate the Communist union. The union was slowly coming apart, an outcome of perestroika and glasnost that Gorbachev had not expected.

According to Jonathan Steele, "By the spring of 1991 Gorbachev was caught between two powerful trends which were narrowing his room for [maneuver]. On one side conservatives and reactionaries in the party were trying to reverse his policies; on the other were progressives who wanted to establish a full multi-party system and take the country towards market reforms."[3]

Gorbachev settled upon a new path: he was close to signing a new treaty with the rebellious nations, which would allow them civil and political independence while leaving them formally allied with the Soviet Union. The treaty was set to be officially signed in August 1991.

The August Coup

However, trouble erupted a few days before the signing. The final blow was dealt in August 1991, while Gorbachev was on vacation in Crimea. A coup d'état to unseat him from power was attempted in Moscow. The coup was led by members of the Communist Party who opposed Gorbachev's reforms and firmly believed that his programs and ideas were weakening the Soviet Union.

Leaders of the coup—eight men altogether, who would later be known as the Gang of Eight—met in the Kremlin during Gorbachev's absence and signed an agreement, declaring a state of emergency and naming Gennady Yanayev the acting president of the Soviet Union. The news was broadcast all over the media, where it was met with shock by Soviet citizens.

Few people understood at first what was happening because the reason offered for the state of emergency was that Gorbachev was allegedly ill. In truth, Gorbachev was still in Crimea, with his wife and daughter and his daughter's family, trapped in his vacation home. A group of men prevented him from leaving, effectively placing him under house arrest. Years later, Gorbachev would say that his life was in danger. "They wanted to provoke me into a fight and even a shootout and that could have resulted in my death," he explained.[4]

Boris Yeltsin was the president of the Russian republic at the time. He publicly declared that a coup had taken place, and he urged the Soviet military not to participate in the coup. Tanks had gathered in Red Square, and the

During an attempted coup, Boris Yeltsin climbed on a military tank and famously addressed protestors, demanding that the people retain their democratic right to choose their leaders.

• •

military had moved in to quell the uprising and civil resistance that was underway.

The military's tank division declared that it would follow Yeltsin's orders, and Yeltsin climbed on top of a tank and made a dramatic speech to the crowd.

Another segment of the military, which was loyal to Yanayev, decided to attack the government building in Moscow. Three protestors were killed in trying to stop the advance on the building, and many other people were injured. This setback caused the troops to stop their advance and withdraw from Moscow, and the coup leaders attempted to meet with Gorbachev in Crimea.

An Excerpt of Boris Yeltsin's Speech

"Citizens of Russia: On the night of 18-19 August 1991, the legally elected president of the country was removed from power.

Regardless of the reasons given for his removal, we are dealing with a rightist, reactionary, anti-constitutional coup. Despite all the difficulties and severe trials being experienced by the people, the democratic process in the country is acquiring an increasingly broad sweep and an irreversible character.

The peoples of Russia are becoming masters of their destiny. The uncontrolled powers of unconstitutional organs have been considerably limited, and this includes party organs. [. . .]

We considered and consider that such methods of force are unacceptable. They discredit the union in the eyes of the whole world, undermine our prestige in the world community, and return us to the Cold War era along with the Soviet Union's isolation in the world community. All of this forces us to proclaim that the so-called committee's ascendancy to power is unlawful.

Accordingly we proclaim all decisions and instructions of this committee to be unlawful.

We are confident that the organs of local power will unswervingly adhere to constitutional laws and decrees of the president of Russia.

We appeal to citizens of Russia to give a fitting rebuff to the putschists and demand a return of the country to normal constitutional development. [. . .]"[5]

When they arrived, Gorbachev refused to negotiate or even to meet with them.

The coup fizzled out after two chaotic days, and Gorbachev was restored to office, although his credibility was severely damaged. The Communist Party was disbanded itself, and the coup leaders were arrested for their actions. A funeral for the three men killed was attended by thousands of Moscow's citizens, and the three were honored posthumously for their bravery.

The true heroes of the day were Boris Yeltsin and the people of Moscow, who had stood up to the forces of corruption. It was Yeltsin who had encouraged the mass uprising that had eventually thwarted the coup.

Taking advantage of his massive popularity and Gorbachev's diminishing powers, Yeltsin effectively began to break Russia—the Soviet Union's largest state—away from the Soviet Union. Gorbachev could do nothing to stop it. By mid-December 1991, Russia had essentially seceded—after that, there was nothing left of the Soviet Union. Yeltsin and other leaders formed a new union, the Commonwealth of Independent States (CIS), and there was nothing left for Gorbachev to do but to resign his own position and dissolve the Soviet Union.

In his speech, delivered in Moscow, Gorbachev implied that he simply had not had enough time to implement the reforms he had introduced:

> All this change had taken a lot of strain, and took place in the context of fierce struggle against the background of increasing resistance by the reactionary forces, both the party and state structures, and the economic elite, as well as our habits, ideological bias, the sponging

attitudes. The change ran up against our intolerance, a low level of political culture and fear of change. That is why we have wasted so much time. The old system fell apart even before the new system began to work."[6]

This statement here means that the new, reformed Soviet Union—the more democratized and open union Gorbachev had envisioned—had simply not had enough time to be fully and completely realized. The problems triggered by disrupting the old system of corruption and bureaucracy had been too overwhelming. According to Robert V. Daniels, perhaps the collapse of the Soviet Union was inevitable, and perhaps even the method by which it collapsed was inevitable. He writes, "Maybe Gorbachev's reform project was doomed from the outset, given the economic difficulties and ethnic-minority grievances in the Soviet Union that he inherited. Maybe, as so many

Russia

Russia is currently the world's largest nation, and it was always the center of the Soviet Union's empire. It is a land rich in natural resources, such as oil, natural gas, and timber. Its coastline extends along the Arctic Ocean and the Pacific Ocean, and it has thousands of water resources, such as rivers and lakes. The Russian people have a long and fascinating history and cultural heritage; there are over 150 ethnic groups in Russia and over 100 languages spoken, although the primary one is Russian, which is a Slavic language.

people have argued in hindsight, the Communist system could not be reformed and could only be demolished by revolution."[7]

Putin During the Collapse of the USSR

Where was Putin during the time that the Soviet Union was collapsing?

When Yeltsin rose to power and successfully broke Russia away from the all-mighty Soviet Union, Putin was living in Leningrad, where he was working in the office of the mayor.

It should not come as a surprise that Putin had a personal connection to the new mayor. He was Anatoly Sobchak, Putin's law professor and mentor at Leningrad State University. In the mayoral election that brought Sobchak to office, the people also voted to restore the city's name to its original one, St. Petersburg, which indicated a distancing from Russia's Soviet influence.

Putin served his former mentor faithfully. With his experience abroad, Putin was the new head of the mayor's foreign relations committee. He learned many things about the inner workings of government, in a time when the Soviet Union and Russia were undergoing historic and often chaotic changes.

Based on remarks he would make years later, it seems Putin believed that the dismantling of the Soviet Union was a disaster. In 2005, during a speech delivered to the Russian parliament, Putin stated, "The collapse of the Soviet Union was the greatest geopolitical catastrophe of the century." He added that, "for the Russian people, it became a real drama. Tens of millions of our citizens

Putin had close ties with Anatoly Sobchak, his law professor and mentor at Leningrad State University. As mayor, Sobchak now helped open the door for Putin to launch his own political career.

and compatriots found themselves outside the Russian Federation."[8] Later, he clarified that he did not miss the days of corrupt bureaucracy and suppression of civil rights; rather, he explained, he thought that the swiftness of the collapse had been damaging to the average Russian person.

> "The collapse of the Soviet Union was the greatest geopolitical catastrophe of the century."[9]

Years later, he also stated that he felt the collapse of the Soviet Union could have been avoided. In 2016, he said, in a speech at the Kremlin, "You know how I feel about the collapse of the Soviet Union, it absolutely wasn't inevitable. A transformation was possible, including of a democratic nature."[10] In other words, he believed that the reforms proposed by Gorbachev could have been successful in opening up the nature of the Soviet government, perhaps even returning the Soviet Union back to Lenin's original ideal of democratic centralism.

Boris Yeltsin

Putin continued to be involved in local politics in St. Petersburg in the early 1990s. By 1994, he assumed the role of first deputy chairman of the St. Petersburg city government and head of external relations for the city.

Anatoly Sobchak lost power in 1996. Anatoly Chubais, a Russian businessman, recommended Putin for a job at the Kremlin. Chubais was Yeltsin's chief of staff and hired Putin to be part of the administration to help move its agenda forward.

Therefore, in 1996, Putin made another move—this time to Moscow. He was appointed to serve as the first deputy manager for the Russian president, Boris Yeltsin, the hero of the August coup. Over the next couple of years, he was promoted and assigned bigger and more influential roles. By 1998, Putin was residential first deputy chief of staff in charge of Russian regions for Yeltsin.

At this time, Yeltsin began to falter as leader, at a time when a strong leader was most needed. In fact, he never

As director of the Russian Federal Security Service, Putin enjoyed greater access to Boris Yeltsin, who came to trust and rely on him. This was an important step in the ambitious Putin's career.

regained the popularity he had in 1991, when he had stood on the tanks in Moscow, condemned the coup, and encouraged the people to rise up in protest. As president of Russia, Yeltsin did not become the democratic leader his people hoped he would be. Instead, he developed a public persona that was not very flattering.

Addicted to alcohol, Yeltsin was loud and belligerent, often doing things that were unthinkable for world leaders. According to Reuters, "In 1992, he played the spoons, a popular musical instrument in Russia, on the head of Askar Akayev, the president of ex-Soviet Kyrgyzstan."[11] Once in Berlin, during a military parade, a drunk Yeltsin grabbed the baton from the orchestra leader and proceeded to outlandishly "conduct" the orchestra himself. According to Daniels, Yeltsin was also addicted to power: "He was addicted to insulting people and bossing them around (a habit naturally cultivated in his early career in the Communist Party apparatus). And he was jealous of any popular subordinate."[12]

There was one young man, however, who was becoming more and more important to Yeltsin— Vladimir Putin.

CHAPTER FOUR

Putin's Rise to Politics

· · · · · · · · · · · · · · ·

One of the missteps that Yeltsin made during his presidency, according to many historians, was the 1994 invasion of Chechnya.

Chechnya was a republic of the Soviet Union, incorporated into the Soviet empire in 1858. Since that time, the Chechens had been punished brutally by Stalin and other Soviet leaders, and they sought independence. They finally saw an opportunity when the Soviet Union collapsed in 1991; immediately the Communist leader was overthrown and Dzhokhar Dudayev, its new president, declared Chechnya free of Russian rule.

However, Chechnya's government was weak. The country was plagued by fighting and grabs for power, as well as by ethnic divisions between Chechens and non-Chechens. Steven Eke, writing for the BBC, noted, "It was a centre of crime, including the trade in arms, drugs and people."[1] Concerned about such a conflict at its borders, Russia decided to invade the small country.

In December 1994, Russian troops entered Chechnya. The war lasted two years, and in the end, Russia was humiliated, having been untrained and unprepared for the unpredictable Chechen guerrilla resistance forces. Up to one hundred thousand people—many of them civilians—were killed. Eke explains that the resistance to the Russian military was fierce: "The result was indiscriminate slaughter. Serious human rights violations, including torture and summary executions, were commonplace."[2]

In the Battle of Grozny, approximately forty thousand Russian troops entered the Chechen capital to squash a revolt. The Chechens drove the Russians from their land and declared freedom.

The war culminated with the Battle of Grozny. During the war, the Russian air force leveled the Chechen city of Grozny, smashing buildings and killing scores of civilians. A year later, the Chechen rebels had regrouped and returned, determined to oust the Russian army. It seemed impossible, but as Michael Specter wrote, "The Chechens . . . [were] pursuing a centuries-old vow to drive the occupiers from their land."[3]

Eventually, the Russians had to surrender and leave Chechnya, humiliated and defeated. The defeat was especially demoralizing because Russia had seen itself as the heir to the Soviet empire. In the end, it had to admit it was not as strong as it had believed.

By this time, Vladimir Putin was part of Boris Yeltsin's inner circle, and he was most likely taking note of how the president had been publicly humiliated by this defeat.

Yeltsin's Favorite

One of Boris Yeltsin's primary advisers was Yevgeny Primakov, who had formerly been part of Mikhail Gorbachev's presidential council. Primakov had also been deeply involved with the KGB, and after the August 1991 attempted coup, he helped reorganize the intelligence organization. Under Primakov, it was renamed the Foreign Intelligence Service, although many agree that it retained its structure and methods. Furthermore, in the first few years after the Soviet Union collapsed, Primakov was viewed by many in Russia as a good negotiator who understood that Russia needed to

Russia's System of Government

In Russia, the government's role is divided among three branches of government: the executive, the legislative, and the judicial.

The president is the person who determines the country's policies and priorities. He or she sits above the three branches of government and directs the military. The president has the authority to appoint a prime minister, but the Russian parliament (the legislative branch) has the ability to approve the decision and to ensure that the person selected is agreeable to them.

The prime minister is the head of the executive branch. His or her role is to implement the details of the policies shaped by the president. In other words, the president makes the major decisions, while the prime minister makes them a reality. The prime minister oversees the other government ministers, who handle various other aspects of government. For example, there is a minister of agriculture, a minister of education, etc.

reassert its authority and its important role in the world community.

In 1996, he became the prime minister of Russia, working closely with Yeltsin. However, in May 1999, he was fired by Yeltsin, who, as president, had the power to remove the Russian prime minister. Yeltsin was being criticized for the fact that the Russian economy had not improved under his leadership, and so he hoped to offset some of the blame onto Primakov. Robert V. Daniels explains that Yeltsin, however, had failed to do anything to solve the real problem. Primakov was a "wily, seasoned ex-spy and arguably the best of Yeltsin's five prime ministers . . . Yeltsin used and discarded subordinates without a second thought. Meanwhile, old Soviet officials gladly supported him while they grabbed public assets—anything from retail shops to the oil industry—and transformed themselves into capitalists while inflation was decimating the incomes and savings of ordinary people."[4]

Indeed, under Yeltsin, corruption continued to grow and the Russian people were becoming more and more financially destitute. While they no doubt had more political freedoms, they were victims of rising crime and unemployment rates.

With Primakov out of the picture, Vladimir Putin was elevated in the government. Always ambitious, he welcomed the opportunity to make himself more influential. He became director of the Federal Security Service in 1998 and, later, was named secretary of the Security Council.

In 1999, Boris Yeltsin disbanded his entire government, shocking
the nation. He named Putin prime minister and acting president.
Putin was eventually elected president of Russia in 2000.

Putin, however, was only one of many voices to whom Yeltsin listened. Many other ministers were also wielding their power over the Russian president, whose days, it seemed increasingly clear, were numbered. It was becoming commonplace to read newspaper reports of his erratic and unstable behavior, which seemed to be worsening even though the country needed him to be firm and controlled. Yeltsin often went into rages. He fired people in his cabinet in a seemingly random way, without much thought. And he seemed disconnected from the very real problems that average Russians were facing. In less than two years, he had fired four prime ministers. It was clear that Yeltsin wouldn't last in office much longer.

His daughter, Tatiana Yeltsina, was able to influence him. Yeltsina, whose last name is now Yumasheva, "had wielded huge and unaccountable power from behind her father's tottering throne for years," according to reporter Andrew Osborn. "During her father's time in office, Ms. Yumasheva helped mastermind government reshuffles and was the key player in an influential group of advisers known as 'The Family.'"[5] It has been reported that Vladimir Putin himself was a member of "The Family."

It was Tatiana who insisted that her father select Putin as his successor, not because Putin was unique or especially influential but because he was in the right place at the right time. Yeltsin had to step down, and Putin was available and willing.

On August 9, 1999, Putin had a momentous day. Yeltsin disbanded his government, firing his latest prime minister, Sergei Stepashin, who had been in the position for only three months. The BBC reported "Mr. Yeltsin also sacked the entire Russian Government,

> "**I shall definitely stand for the post of Russian president.**"[7]

but has asked the cabinet to stay on temporarily."[6] The move stunned the world and seemed like one of Yeltsin's latest erratic actions; the value of the ruble, the Russian currency, plunged with this latest uncertainty.

That same day, Yeltsin also named Putin Russia's new prime minister. And then he did something even more incredible: he went one step further by announcing that Putin would also be his successor as president. Responding to Yeltsin's announcement, Putin stated, "'I shall definitely stand for the post of Russian president."[8]

Putin's Appeal

Putin was not received warmly when Yeltsin made his startling announcement on August 9, 1999. It surprised some others in the Russian government to see that Putin had become the favorite, but it seems that Tatiana Yeltsina and "The Family" were behind this selection.

However, Putin did win the approval of the Russian parliament, winning more votes than was needed. Perhaps the legislators did not think he would last long, given that he was the fifth prime minister to be appointed in such a short time. He was approved on August 16, 1999.

The Russian people seemed to like their new prime minister, perhaps because of the stark contrast to Yeltsin himself. Whereas Yeltsin was an alcoholic and erratic, Putin was very disciplined—he controlled himself carefully, was physically fit and athletic, and was very orderly in all of his affairs. He spoke directly and simply, which also appealed to the people.

Even though he had been seen as a hard-working and efficient minister, and a loyalist to Yeltsin, Putin now seemed to pose a challenge to other politicians who hoped to rise in the government. Yeltsin had declared that Putin was his favorite to succeed him as president, but Yeltsin's opinions changed almost weekly. Those who saw Putin as competition attempted to diminish his high rank in Yeltsin's favor.

Second Chechen War

In September 1999, Russia invaded Chechnya, launching the Second Chechen War. The invasion was apparently prompted by the invasion of neighboring Dagestan by Chechen rebels in August.

> "It is obvious that in these conditions we must think about ensuring our own security."[9]

However, the story is more complicated than that. While Chechens did invade Dagestan, it was a series of bombings in Russia itself that stirred up popular support for an attack on Chechnya. According to the *World Affairs Journal*, "A series of apartment

Yeltsin and Scandal

Boris Yeltsin was no stranger to scandal. A bribery scandal that emerged in late 1999 was probably the reason why he suddenly resigned his post as president of Russia, and many people surmise that he chose Putin as his successor because Putin agreed not to pursue charges against him.

According to the BBC, investigators in Switzerland claimed that the Mabetex construction company bribed Yeltsin and his two daughters, giving the Russian first family approximately $15 million. Mabetex, in exchange, wanted to earn construction contracts from the Kremlin, which would have been clearly illegal for Yeltsin to do—that is, to personally benefit by giving government contracts.

The BBC report states, "Swiss investigators say they have evidence that President Yeltsin and his two daughters were provided with credit cards and the bill was met by Mabetex."[10]

bombings struck three Russian cities, killing almost 300 people. The Kremlin was quick to blame Chechens, but when an unexploded bomb was found in a fourth city, the perpetrators turned out to be Russian agents. Putin, nevertheless, sent troops to the restive Muslim republic, creating a wave of patriotic fervor that swept him to power."[11]

When Boris Yeltsin left office in 1999, he still had several months left in his term. Putin was named acting president until elections could be held.

• •

Was the case for invading Chechnya planted? It remains unclear, but it is very certain that "Putin made his name from his response"[12] to the Dagestan invasion. The war was seen by many in Russia as one that was handled effectively, with Chechen militants defeated. This victory was attributed to Putin's planning and strategy. His reputation grew as a leader who could get things done in the corrupt, complicated system of Russian politics.

Putin now seemed very powerful indeed, and his competitors wanted to stop his ascent.

However, they were too late: on December 31, 1999, Boris Yeltsin officially—and suddenly—resigned from office. He had been under investigation for a bribery scandal, in which he and his family were suspected of accepting bribes from a construction and engineering firm.

Russia's constitution provides for the scenario of a president's resignation; the prime minister becomes the acting president until an election can be held.

On December 31, Vladimir Putin, the steady, disciplined, former KGB spy, became the acting president of Russia. One of his first actions, on that day, was to agree not to allow the government to pursue an investigation against Yeltsin or his family.

CHAPTER FIVE

President Putin

. . . .

On March 26, 2000, Russia held elections, and the people voted for Vladimir Putin as the second democratically elected president of Russia. Putin won slightly more than 50 percent of the vote. His opponent was Gennady Zyuganov, who later claimed that Putin had falsified the election results, but it seemed clear that the Russian people were attracted to Putin's message. During the months before the election, Putin had pledged to focus his efforts on fixing Russia's economy.

Why did he win? What did the Russian people see in him?

It seems odd, given Putin's bleak public persona. In the days when he was serving in Boris Yeltsin's inner circle, Putin was overlooked as a real contender. A BBC report explains, "Far from charismatic, he has an expressionless mask-like face, rarely smiles, and speaks softly . . . For years [Putin] had a reputation as a 'grey cardinal,' a man who wields power quietly, behind the scenes."[1] This last comment has been reported in other sources—Putin was quietly gaining power but remaining quiet, a skill perhaps learned in his years spent as a spy in East Germany.

Were the Russian people not turned off by his lack of charisma, which is known to be an essential skill for all politicians?

Again, they seem to have been captured by what he was not, rather than what he was. Putin was not Yeltsin. In fact, he was starkly different than his predecessor. He was a judo expert. He remained calm under pressure. He had excellent oratory skills. He was a "strong man"— someone who believed in law and order and brought a sort of tough, effective edge to the position.

An article in the *Nation* noted, "Putin's difference from Yeltsin appealed to most Russians: Putin was consistent, stern, steady, a leader who brought 'certainty' to a country constantly thrown off balance by Yeltsin's erratic behavior."[2]

He was also much younger than Yeltsin and some of the other Russian leaders. Michael McFaul, former US ambassador to Russia under President Barack Obama, states, "His youth and energy also punctuated the end of an old and sick ruler at the top. The voters welcomed this generational change. In focus groups that I commissioned in December 1999 and March 2000, Russian voters uniformly stated that Putin's youth was a positive attribute."[3]

Did people worry about his closeness to Yeltsin, who was known to be corrupt? Did they fear, as many in the

West did, that Putin would crack down on individual civil and political rights of Russian citizens?

The answer is no. Putin seemed to embrace a desire to move Russia toward democratic reform, even though his main priority would be the economy.

He was sworn into office that May. In his acceptance speech, he referred to his predecessor:

> I am aware that I have undertaken a huge responsibility and I am aware that the head of state in Russia has always been and will always be responsible for everything, for everything that is happening in the country. On leaving the Kremlin, the first president of Russia, Boris Nikolayevich Yeltsin, made remarks which many would remember. He reminded us of these words today. He said and repeated in this hall today: take care of Russia. This is how I see my main task as president.[4]

Other nations, such as the United States, acknowledge that the process of a fair election in Russia was a big advancement. In his testimony before the Senate Foreign Relations Committee, Michael McFaul stated, "For the first time in Russia's history, power within the Kremlin changed hands through an electoral process. The election did occur and was conducted as prescribed by the constitution, no small achievements for a country with Russia's authoritarian history. More than two-thirds of the eligible voters participated, and they appeared to make informed choices between a range of candidates who offered alternative platforms, policies, and leadership styles."[5]

Nevertheless, McFaul and others felt that while Putin talked about democratic reform, it was uncertain that

Putin was inaugurated as president of Russia on May 7, 2000. His inauguration was held in St. Andrew Hall of the Grand Kremlin Palace in Moscow. Boris Yeltsin was in attendance.

he would lead Russia in that direction. For example, the way he came to power was not entirely fair. McFaul points out that Yeltsin and "The Family" selected Putin as the successor because he would keep them from being prosecuted for corruption, and, he wrote, "To get him elected, they had to provoke a war with Chechnya as a way to boost Putin's popularity."[6]

An Excerpt from Vladimir Putin's Inauguration Speech

Today is truly a historic day. I wish to focus attention on this once more. In actual fact, for the first time in the entire history of our state, for the first time in Russian history, supreme power in the country is handed over in the most democratic and in the most simple way: through the will of the people—legally and peacefully.

The transfer of power is always a test of the constitutional system, a test of its strength.

It is true that this is not the first test for us. Perhaps, it is not the last one.

However, we have gone through this trial, this stage, with dignity. We have proved that Russia is becoming a truly democratic modern state. The peaceful succession of power is the crucial element of the political stability which we have dreamt of, to which we have aspired and which we have sought.[7]

While these questions about how Russia would fare with its new leader at the helm, Putin, as president, now sat above the three branches of Russia's government: the legislative, the executive, and the judicial.

A Strong Russia

Right away, Putin seemed interested in reasserting the reputation of Russia as a strong nation and a key player in world affairs. One way he could do that was to challenge the current world superpower, the United States, which had been, in many ways, alone at the top.

In June 2000, he met with US president Bill Clinton in a summit held in Moscow. The two men signed an arms control agreement, but they did not see eye to eye on the United States government's plans to build a national missile defense shield. Worried about possible missile attacks from North Korea or Middle Eastern nations, Clinton wanted to deploy missile interceptors around the globe. The strategy required Russia's agreement to the plan because of a previous treaty between the two countries. However, Putin disliked this idea because it would reveal his country's weakness. As Douglas Waller explains: "The U.S. wants Russia to amend the 1972 Anti-Ballistic Missile Treaty to allow for the deployments. Russia's military can't afford to build a shield in response, so Putin balks at any tinkering with the accord."[9]

> "We have a common goal: a strong Russia."[8]

Putin welcomed US president Bill Clinton to Moscow in June 2000. The summit between the two leaders led to the signing of an arms control agreement.

• •

In an effort to stymie Clinton's plans, Putin energetically condemned the idea of the missile shield in discussions with other world leaders. He made a diplomatic trip to China, where he and Chinese president Jiang Zemin issued a joint statement in which they criticized Clinton's idea. Finally, President Clinton abandoned the plan, deciding to leave it to the next

American president—who would be elected later that year—to decide.

In Russia, Clinton's decision was seen as a victory for Putin, who was portrayed as a tough negotiator and a man who could make Russia a powerful player in world politics once again. After all, he had taken on the American president, and technically he had won. One Russian official was quoted as saying, "This enables Putin to say that his firm stand on the ABM Treaty has been vindicated and that Clinton listened to his arguments."[10]

While Clinton likely had other reasons for delaying the decision on the missile shield program, Putin's popularity soared, despite the fact that, as president, he had started to clamp down on the Russian media. Later, Clinton famously said that while Putin seemed like an honorable man with good intentions for Russia, "He could get squishy on democracy."[11]

A National Tragedy

In August 2000, President Putin faced a major national crisis. A Russian submarine, the *Kursk*, was in trouble, and the lives of its sailors were in peril. One of the most impressive vessels in the Russian navy, the *Kursk* was supposed to be "unsinkable." A massive submarine the size of two jumbo jets, "it could even withstand a direct hit from a torpedo attack."[13]

> "We shall not allow the national pride of Russians to be trod upon . . . We are sure of the power and prosperity of our country."[12]

However, on August 12, 2000, while the *Kursk* was conducting a military exercise in the Barents Sea, a major explosion was registered, followed by a second smaller one. The *Kursk* began to sink and crashed onto the bottom of the sea.

The fate of the 118 Russians aboard the submarine was unknown for a long time, as it took the Russian navy several hours to understand the full danger that the *Kursk* was in and eventually to locate it. For four days, the Russian navy tried to rescue the men onboard, employing different tactics to no avail. In the meantime, as the Russian people became more and more alarmed at the news, the Russian government seemed to mask what was really happening and to hide the truth from its own citizens. Initially, the accident was blamed on a collision with a NATO submarine, but this was found to be untrue.

The family members of the *Kursk* crew members became frantic with fear and were shown on international media, becoming more and more agitated and worried as time was running out. Meanwhile, President Putin was on a vacation at a Russian seaside resort and did not cut short his trip, despite mounting criticism. Later, he claimed that navy officials had told him that the situation and the rescue efforts were under control.

Foreign nations offered Putin the help of their navy and rescue teams, but Putin refused, believing that the men would be rescued soon by the Russians themselves.

There was hope. Divers had heard tapping messages, done in code, from men who were still alive inside,

A memorial was built in honor of several of the Russian sailors who died aboard the *Kursk*. The submarine sank on August 12, 2000. The tragedy shocked the nation, who grieved the loss of 118 sailors.

indicating that they were trapped and running out of air. "SOS—water" the tapping indicated.

However, after five days without success—and the fate of 118 men still unknown—the Russian rescue effort fell apart. On August 17, Putin accepted international help. British and Norwegian rescue teams arrived the next day and sent a rescue submarine into the Barents Sea. After a

Final Words from the *Kursk*

Investigations into the sinking of the *Kursk* later revealed that while many of the crew had died in the initial explosions, many others had survived and crowded into the vessel's escape hatch. They tried to exit the vessel, but the escape hatch itself was damaged and could not be opened.

In one of the incident's most devastating aspects, it appears that these men realized they were not going to survive. They wrote messages to their families and loved ones, saying good-bye.

One message was found on the body of Lieutenant-Captain Dmitri Kolesnikov, who was twenty-seven years old. Most of his message was not revealed to the public, as it was intended only for his family and for his wife, Olga.

The part that was revealed explained why the surviving men had left their posts to gather in the *Kursk*'s ninth compartment. The note stated: "It's 13:15. All personnel from section six, seven and eight have moved to section nine. There are 23 people here. We have made the decision because none of us can escape. I am writing this blind."[14]

few more days, they were finally able to access the escape hatch of the *Kursk*.

To everyone's dismay and horror, the Russian navy announced, on August 21, that none of the crew members of the *Kursk* had survived the ordeal. Some had died during the initial explosion, while others had drowned or died of hypothermia when the escape hatch had flooded.

On August 22, Putin held a private meeting with the families of the *Kursk* crew members. Reporters who posed as family members and attended the meeting said that Putin apologized to the several hundred people gathered and that the family members screamed and shouted at him, demanding to know why he had waited so long to accept help. It was, by these accounts, a contentious and emotional meeting that lasted several hours.

The *Kursk* affair cast doubt on Putin's leadership and his ability to see logically past Russia's weaknesses. Had he realized sooner, critics said, that Russia's navy was unable to handle the crisis, he would have accepted help, rather than insist that Russia could handle it alone. Writing for the *Guardian*, Marcus Warren reported, "The press has shown no mercy in denouncing Mr Putin's performance and the military's conduct. Typical headlines read, 'The reputation of the Russian leadership is lying on the bottom of the Barents Sea' and 'Nine days of national shame.'"[15]

Putin remained calm and steady, showing little emotion. However, the patriarch of the Russian Orthodox Church attested that Putin was also emotionally suffering: "I have seen with what pain the president is living through this crisis."[16]

Not long after the tragedy, Putin's government re-established control over the state television media, a move that many said was intended to consolidate his power and silence his critics.

CHAPTER SIX

Putin Invades the Crimea

· · · · · · · · · · · · · · · · · · · ·

Despite the *Kursk* incident and the way in which his critics condemned his failure to act swiftly during that crisis, Putin remained generally popular throughout Russia. One of the main reasons for this was that the nation's economy was improving steadily. Russia is a primary exporter of gas and oil, and oil prices around the world were increasing. In fact, in terms of oil production, Russia nearly caught up with the production rates of powerhouse Saudi Arabia.

The improved economy helped many Russians stabilize their family situations. After the collapse of the Soviet Union, the country's population had been on a steep decline, at the astounding rate of one million people a year. This was because people were dying young and couples were not having children. In addition, the immigration rate was low. However, this population trend began to reverse in the early 2000s. According to the *Guardian*, "The secret to this reversal was largely economic: as their financial situation improved during Putin's reign, Russians began having more children."[1]

Dubrovka Theater Siege

Russians also may have had confidence in their leader because Putin handled major crises in ways that displayed strength and steadiness. One such crisis occurred on October 23, 2002, when forty Chechen militants stormed into the Dubrovka Theater in Moscow, holding the 912 occupants inside hostage. The Chechen militants demanded that Russia withdraw its troops from Chechnya. If the Russian government didn't comply, they said, they would blow up the theater. Indeed the forty Chechen militants—both men and women—had in their possession explosives and bombs.

Three days after the initial takeover of the theater, Russian forces pumped a sleeping gas, an opiod substance, into the theater. This served to knock out everyone inside. The Russian police then entered the theater, shooting the militants. The hostages were carried out—most of them still asleep—although it became clear, very quickly, that many of them had died as a result of the gas. Doctors on the scene were not informed of the type of gas that had been used, so efforts to save them were futile. In fact, the specific type of gas used was kept secret by the Russian police, even though, at the end, 130 hostages died as a result. According to the *Atlantic*, "Relatives of the victims pin the blame squarely on President Vladimir Putin, who they say gave the orders to use the poisonous gas and helped cover up the deadly rescue operation."[2]

Relatives of the dead hostages sued the government for botching the rescue mission and killing their loved ones, but their claim was rejected in the courts. While many say the Dubrovka Theater crisis soiled Putin's image again, many Russians also sympathized with his situation, perhaps as a result of anti-Chechen fear and resentment.

Beslan School Siege

Chechen militants struck again, this time in 2004. In August of that year, suicide bombers caused the crashes

One hundred and thirty hostages died during the standoff at the Dubrovka Theater. This photo depicts a special forces officer carrying a woman out of the Moscow theater.

of two Russian passenger jets. Then, on September 1, approximately thirty armed militants took over a school in the Russian city of Beslan. It was the school's opening day, and one thousand students, teachers, and parents who were there for opening ceremonies were taken hostage. They were all crowded into the school's gymnasium, and large bombs were rigged to the basketball goals inside the gym. The Chechens' demand was the same as it had been two years earlier: the withdrawal of Russia from the Chechen republic.

After two days, explosions—their source unknown—went off inside the school, and gunfire ensued. Russian commandos stormed the building as some hostages tried to flee and were shot at by the militants. In the chaos, the roof of the gymnasium collapsed, killing many people inside. By the end of the siege, 330 people died, including 186 children. The victims had been killed by militant gunfire or by being crushed by the roof collapse.

The grief throughout Russia and around the world was palpable. People reeled from the tremendous loss of life, even as critics charged the Russian police force with once again botching a rescue operation. Putin responded by centralizing the government's power. He took steps to cancel elections for governors in Russia's republics. Instead, he decided, these governors would be directly appointed by him as a way for him to better control the country. His actions were condemned as anti-democratic, as a way to exploit the crisis to seize more and more power.

Terrorists took over a school in Beslan, Russia, in 2004, demanding the withdrawal of Russian forces from Chechnya. Russian commandos stormed the school, and altogether, 385 people died.

Revolution in Ukraine

One of Putin's boldest moves happened in Ukraine, when he annexed the peninsula known as Crimea and "re-claimed" it for Russia.

In 1991, when the Soviet Union collapsed, Ukraine was one of the countries that had voted to be independent from the former empire. In fact, in the referendum vote that was held, approximately 90 percent of Ukrainians voted for independence.

Separating from the Soviet Union, and from Russia, would not be that simple, however. In Ukraine, there was still a significant faction of people who wanted to remain loyal to Russia and to be allied with Boris Yelstin's government. In fact, the country was almost divided in that respect. According to William Schneider, writing in the *Atlantic*, "Ukraine's east is mostly Russian-speaking, Orthodox in religion, and strongly pro-Russian. Most people in Ukraine's west speak Ukrainian and adhere to a church that acknowledges the authority of the Roman Catholic pope. Western Ukrainians are intensely nationalistic and distrustful of Russia."[3]

In 2004, as Ukraine moved slowly toward democratic reform, the Orange Revolution took place. Politician Viktor Yushchenko protested an election in which the winner was his opponent, the pro-Russian prime minister Viktor Yanukovych. The election was criticized as having been tainted or rigged in Yanukovych's favor. Civil protests and mass demonstrations erupted. People filled the main square in the capital city of Kiev, chanting *"Razom nas bahato! Nas ne podolaty!"* which means "Together, we are many! We cannot be defeated!"[4] The

Yushchenko's Speech About Freedom

A 2005 speech by Viktor Yushchenko seemed to indicate that the country was finally moving toward real democratic reform:

Dear Ukrainians: I want to say the main thing!

I am convinced we will unveil our potential. And we should know that prosperity cannot be presented on a platter. The country's progress, freedom, democracy and welfare are made by millions of hands. All of us will have to work hard. We should be firm, single-minded, united and respectful of each other. That is how we won a victory on the maidan and how we will win in the future.

We have every reason to speak about our prospects. Only a strong nation could have changed the country so radically over the last months. Today we speak about Ukraine, very often using the phrase "for the first time."

For the first time we can express our ideas freely. There are no issues and persons forbidden for the media. A journalist criticizing the authorities risks neither his or her work nor life. Freedom of speech—the alpha and omega of democracy—has become a reality in Ukraine. We have an opportunity to breathe freely, and we are now learning to do it.[5]

protestors wore orange and held up orange banners—Yushchenko's campaign colors.

During the revolution, there was an assassination attempt on the life of Yushchenko. He was nearly killed after eating soup that had been laced with the poison dioxin. Early reports suggested he had been infected by a virus, but his doctor later clarified for the press: "There is no doubt that Mr. Yushchenko's disease has been caused by a case of poisoning by dioxin. We suspect involvement of an external party, but we cannot answer as to who cooked what or who was with him while he ate."[6] While he survived the poisoning, recovery was slow and Yushchenko was left with a badly scarred and pockmarked face.

Russian operatives were suggested as the culprits, but this was never confirmed. Years later, Yushchenko implied that the assassination was attempted because Russia, under Putin, wanted to maintain its power over Ukraine and to prevent Ukraine from turning toward the European Union. He said, "Every politician in this country and neighbouring countries who turns towards the West is facing that kind of danger. My poisoning took place because I had started taking steps towards the European Union. We have a neighbour who does not want this to happen."[7]

During the revolution, the Ukrainian parliament passed a no-confidence vote in Yanukovych's government. After much turmoil, the judicial branch declared the election results to be void. Yushchenko finally emerged winner of the election in December 2004, and he assumed the office of president.

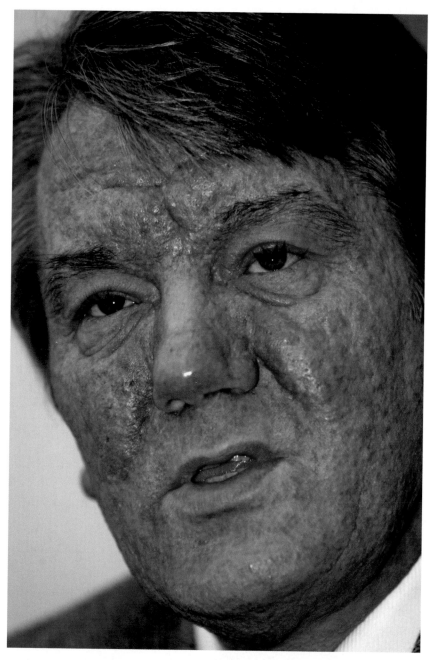

Ukraine's opposition leader Viktor Yushchenko was poisoned in an assassination attempt. Though he survived, the attack left Yushchenko with a badly scarred face.

Things changed in 2010, however, when Yanukovych ran again in the presidential elections, and this time, he won. Under Yanukovych, Ukraine began abandoning ties with the European Union (EU) and, instead, grew closer to Russia, led by Putin. For example, in 2013, Ukraine suddenly backed out of a trade agreement with the European Union, a move that was claimed by critics to be influenced by the Kremlin. A BBC analyst stated, "Russia wants Ukraine to join its own customs union with Kazakhstan and Belarus, which it sees as a prototype rival to the European Union."[8] For pro-Western Ukrainians, it felt like the old days of the Soviets, when their government's decisions were dictated by Russia.

Within a month, protests were underway. In December 2013, people who were rallying against pro-Russian politicians occupied Kiev's city hall building. Yanukovych appealed to Putin, who threw his Ukrainian counterpart "an economic lifeline," as news reports put it, "agreeing to buy $15bn of Ukrainian debt and reduce the price of Russian gas supplies by about a third."[10] This improved Ukraine's economy and made it appear that Russia would be a good partner, but it did not improve the political climate within the country. Protests became deadly as riots erupted. These became only worse when

> **"We [. . .] hoped that all native Russians, the Russian-speaking people living in Ukraine, would live in a comfortable political environment, that they would not be threatened or oppressed."[9]**

What Is the Crimea?

Crimea, sometimes referred to as The Crimea, is a peninsula that sits between Ukraine and Russia on the Black Sea. It is a fascinating intersection of Eastern and Western cultures, of Greek, Russian, Ukrainian, Byzantine, Turkish, and Arab influences. Many Crimeans consider themselves to be distinct from Ukraine, but during the Soviet empire, Crimea was considered part of Ukraine. After the Soviet Union collapsed in 1991, Crimea became an autonomous republic within Ukraine, even though 60 percent of the population is ethnically Russian. As Caroline Mortimer explains, "Crimea is strategically important as a base for the Russian navy. The Black Sea Fleet has been based on the peninsula since it was founded by Prince Potemkin in 1783."[11] It is unlikely that Russia will abandon its occupation of Crimea anytime soon.

parliament attempted to pass an anti-protest law (which was later overturned) and as police brutally suppressed the protests.

On February 20, 2014, police fired into crowds of protestors, and clashes became especially violent. Within two days, approximately eighty-eight people were dead. A turbulent several days followed: Yanukovych seemed to be replaced, and he later claimed that a coup had taken place to oust him. His primary opponent, pro-Western Yulia Tymoshenko (a former ally of Viktor

Yushchenko's), was released from jail. Parliament named Olexander Turchynov as the new interim president and declared that new elections would be held in May.

Showdown over Crimea

Another facet of the turmoil in Ukraine emerged in late February 2014, when pro-Russian gunmen occupied the government buildings of Crimea's capital, Simferopol. Crimea was an autonomous republic of the Ukraine, one that had long been of key interest to Russia because of its position on the Black Sea and its importance as a naval

In 2014, Putin signed a law that made the Crimea a part of Russia. The decision was supported by a referendum vote that was alleged to have been rigged.

base. The presence of pro-Russian militia in Crimea's capital city seemed ominous and the sign of a looming takeover by Russia.

Indeed, Putin made a request of the Russian parliament to use Russian forces to move into Crimea. The parliament approved his request on March 1, using the logic that Russia should protect its interests because of the instability in Ukraine. On March 16, a referendum vote was held in Crimea, on whether the people wanted to secede from Ukraine and join Russia, and it was approved by 97 percent—although

> **"Order in [Ukraine] can only be restored through dialogue and democratic procedures, rather than with the use of armed force, tanks and aircraft."[12]**

this vote was widely denounced as having been rigged by the Russians. On March 18, Putin signed a bill stating that Crimea would be formally returned to the Russian Federation, and he delivered an emotional speech during which he said that Crimea had always been part of Russia, and that it had been unfairly become part of Ukraine during the collapse of the Soviet Union:

Colleagues,

In people's hearts and minds, Crimea has always been an inseparable part of Russia. This firm conviction is based on truth and justice and was passed from generation to generation, over time, under any circumstances, despite all the dramatic changes our country went through during the entire

20th century. [. . .] I heard residents of Crimea say that back in 1991 they were handed over like a sack of potatoes. This is hard to disagree with. And what about the Russian state? What about Russia? It humbly accepted the situation. This country was going through such hard times then that realistically it was incapable of protecting its interests. However, the people could not reconcile themselves to this outrageous historical injustice.[13]

The outcry against Russia's takeover of Crimea was swift. President Barack Obama and Vice President Joe Biden of the United States labeled it a land grab by Russia. The European Union also was clear in its condemnation of the move: "The sovereignty, territorial integrity and independence of Ukraine must be respected. The European Union does neither recognise the illegal and illegitimate referendum in Crimea nor its outcome. The European Union does not and will not recognise the annexation of Crimea and Sevastopol to the Russian Federation."[14] The Western nations—the United States and Europe, especially—believed that Putin's annexation of Crimea was a threat to growing democracy in Europe and an attempt to rob Ukraine of a strategic segment of its country.

The United States and the European Union took action: they imposed sanctions on Russia. The sanctions include banning travel for many key players, such as Crimea's leaders and many Russian leaders who are close to Putin. The sanctions also freeze the assets of those people on the list. This means that the people on the blacklist may not travel to or enter the United States or European nations. It also means that any money or property that they own in American or European banks cannot be accessed. Future arms, technology, and trade deals between the nations are banned, and Russian banks are also limited and face many financial restrictions as a result of the sanctions.

In Russia, however, the move by Putin was generally popular. Russians felt that Putin was restoring and rebuilding Russia and protecting Russia's interests—the Crimea as a place for its naval fleet—against the rest of the world. Many Russians did not view Putin as escalating the problem in Ukraine but rather as making sure that Russia's interests were not eclipsed by an unstable situation in neighboring Ukraine.

Overall, the situation has exacerbated tensions between the United States and the European Union and Russia, and it seems that the world is reverting back to the old division of East versus West.

CHAPTER SEVEN

US Elections

· · · · · · · · · · · · · · · · · · ·

In 2008, Vladimir Putin was constitutionally barred from running for the office of the presidency because he had already served two terms, the limit under Russia's constitution. He announced that he would not run because he planned to abide by the laws of the constitution.

A Putin ally, Dmitry Medvedev, ran for the office of president and won. Medvedev had formerly been a deputy prime minister under Putin. The two men had a common mentor: Anatoly Sobchak. In fact, Medvedev had graduated from the law school of Leningrad State University, just like Putin had.

Despite these connections, the Russian people were nevertheless shocked when, after winning the presidential election, Medvedev appointed as his prime minister none other than Vladimir Putin. This move was criticized by Russians and leaders around the world as a clear attempt by Putin to lead the Russian government, using Medvedev as a "puppet" president.

In 2012, as the next round of presidential elections neared, Medvedev announced that he would not run for a second term. Putin announced that he would run, and he won—by a handy 65 percent of the vote. In addition, the Russian constitution was amended: instead of a presidential term lasting four years, it would now last six years. Charges of fraud and vote-rigging abounded, and between one hundred to two hundred people were arrested for protesting on the day of the inauguration.

In one of his first actions as president in this third term, Putin appointed Medvedev as prime minister, which seemed to confirm the allegations of election manipulation.

Hillary Clinton: An Old Foe

In 2015, the United States embarked on its own election cycle as campaigning began for the 2016 presidential elections. By the summer of 2016, the two major political parties in the United States voted for and nominated their candidates. The Democrats nominated a woman for the first time: former first lady and former secretary of state Hillary Rodham Clinton, who had been first lady for the two terms her husband, Bill, was president. She also had served as secretary of state under President Barack Obama. The Republicans nominated businessman and real estate mogul Donald J. Trump, a newcomer to politics.

In the past, Hillary Clinton had clashed with President Putin on several occasions. As a strong political

Hillary Clinton served as the US secretary of state from 2009 to 2013. Some say Clinton's criticisms of Putin were behind Russia's alleged tampering of the 2016 US presidential election.

• •

negotiator, Clinton openly criticized Putin for being authoritarian and anti-democratic, which irritated him.

In one of her last acts as secretary of state, Clinton wrote a memo for the Obama administration, offering advice on how to handle Putin diplomatically:

> Don't appear too eager to work together. Don't flatter Putin with high-level attention. Decline his invitation for a presidential summit.[1]

She added that Putin had to be handled with a tough stance, not usually reserved for foreign leaders, but "strength and resolve were the only language Putin would understand."[2]

Indeed, Clinton had publicly commented on Russian elections in the past. When protestors filled the streets of Moscow in 2012, Clinton said that the elections had not been fair and open; indeed, many independent election watchers had confirmed that there had been fraudulent activities during that election as well. Clinton said, "The Russian people, like people everywhere, deserve the right to have their voices heard and their votes counted. And that means they deserve fair, free, transparent elections and leaders who are accountable to them."[3] Putin was apparently infuriated by Clinton's comments and felt that he was being personally attacked by a foreign leader.

During the 2016 US campaign, it was clear that Putin preferred that Clinton not win the election. In the summer of 2016, the Democratic National Committee's email systems were hacked, and emails and communications were leaked to the public. These emails contained information that was embarrassing to many people, especially in the Democratic Party, because they indicated that there had been some corruption in how Clinton was nominated.

For example, there was some communication between DNC chairwoman Debbie Wasserman Shultz and other DNC staff members, in which they deliberately planned to diminish the campaign of Vermont senator Bernie Sanders, who was challenging Clinton for the nomination. Sanders's campaign was extremely popular in 2016, leading many people to believe that he might defeat her and win the nomination of the Democratic

Party. The DNC is supposed to remain neutral during the nomination process, allowing Americans to vote for their own party's nominee, but leaked emails showed that this was not the case.

In these emails, Chairwoman Wasserman Shultz indicated that she was trying to promote positive news stories about Hillary Clinton. There was at least one email, from May 2016, showing that another DNC official was trying to highlight Senator Sanders's Jewish background as a way to make him unpopular with Christian voters:

> It may make no difference but for KY and WA can we get someone to ask his belief. He had skated on having a Jewish heritage. I read he is an atheist. This could make several points difference with my peeps. My Southern Baptist peeps would draw a big difference between a Jew and an atheist.[4]

Another email showed that Donna Brazile, who was affiliated with the DNC, also made some unethical moves. In addition to her position within the DNC, Brazile was also a contributor to CNN, the popular cable news television station. CNN hosted a townhall-style debate between Clinton and Sanders. A leaked email proved that Brazile had been shown some of the questions that Sanders and Clinton would be asked, and that she passed along at least one of these questions to Clinton's campaign. In other words, the Russian hack of the DNC emails helped unearth and make public unethical and corrupt behavior that was already occurring—in short, that the DNC was trying very hard to make sure Clinton was the nominee of the Democratic Party.

Cyber Attack

It is almost certain that Vladimir Putin was behind the email hacking. "Cyber warriors" were online, trying to hack into the computers of various DNC staffers, and once they were able to infiltrate one or two, it was easy to obtain the rest. They gave the emails to WikiLeaks as a way of distancing the Russian government from the hacks. WikiLeaks is an organization headed by Julian Assange; its mission is to obtain and publish top-secret correspondence, information, and communications of companies and governments so that the information is in the hands of the people. However, having WikiLeaks, which is known for "dumping" vast amounts of information at a time (that is, making it available online), reveal the information was not quite enough distance—it was obvious that the original sources of the information were Russian hackers, who worked at the command of President Putin.

Jeff Pegues writes, "U.S. intelligence believes the cyber attack on the email of the Democratic National Committee was ordered by Russian President Vladimir Putin,"[5] and the evidence for this comes from a variety of reliable sources in the intelligence community. Barack Obama, who was the president at that point, ordered a full investigation into the hack, which many in the American government believe was a form of an attack on the United States because it interfered with its democratic elections.

Why would Putin do such a thing? According to Andrew Roth and Dana Priest, the hacks are "President Vladimir Putin's splashy response to years of what he sees as U.S. efforts to weaken and shame him on the world stage and with his own people, according to Russia experts here and in the U.S. intelligence world and academia."[6] He probably hoped to make the election cycle chaotic and confusing by revealing the emails, and he wanted to make the campaign of Hillary Clinton seem as unfavorable to American voters as possible.

Russia and "Fake News"

Another question that has arisen in the United States is whether or not certain Americans were aware that Russia was trying to diminish the campaign of Hillary Clinton. Specifically, did the campaign of Donald J. Trump know what was happening, and did members of the Trump campaign work with Russians to win the election?

There are many reasons why this question is being asked. First, during his campaign, Trump, who is now president of the United States, made many favorable comments about President Putin. It was clear that he wanted to be more open-minded toward the Russian leader, which was a change of attitude from the Obama administration's attitude toward Putin. As far back as 2007, Trump had words of praise for Putin:

> "[When asked if Russia had intervened in the US elections] "Read my lips—no."[7]

> Look at Putin—what he's doing with Russia—I mean, you know, what's going on over there. I mean this guy has done—whether you like him or don't like him—he's

Donald Trump won the 2016 presidential election, in an upset over
Democratic nominee Hillary Clinton. Questions about his relationship with Putin have clouded Trump's presidency.

doing a great job in rebuilding the image of Russia and also rebuilding Russia period.[8]

In 2013, Trump, who is fond of using Twitter to communicate his thoughts, tweeted: "Do you think Putin will be going to The Miss Universe Pageant in November in Moscow—if so, will he become my new best friend?"[9] (Trump was the owner of the Miss Universe pageant.) After Putin's widely condemned and controversial annexation of Crimea, Trump tweeted—in a triumphant tone—"I believe Putin will continue to rebuild the Russian Empire. He has zero respect for Obama or the U.S.!"[10] There have been many other comments made by Trump that have shown that he has admiration for Putin as a world leader. Some have speculated that, as a successful businessman, President Trump conducted many business dealings with Russians and has had a friendly relationship with Putin in that regard. However, his favorable comments about Putin's leadership abilities specifically—he has even stated that Putin is a stronger and better leader than former President Obama—have perplexed many Americans, who see so much about Putin's methods that are against American values.

The second reason why there are questions about whether or not the Trump campaign worked with the Russians during the election is the phenomenon of "fake news." For example, on December 4, 2016, a North Carolina man went to the Comet Ping Pong pizza shop in Washington, DC, and fired his gun into the restaurant. Nobody was hurt, but the incident's cause was shocking: The man had read online that DNC officials and Hillary Clinton were operating a child pedophilia ring out of the pizza restaurant. This information, which was quickly proven false, had been circulating in fake news stories on the internet.

Who started these rumors, which had spread quite widely? Intelligence sources believe that the story, which was dubbed PizzaGate, was one of many fake news stories that Russian operatives invented and planted online and in social media platforms so that they would spread far and wide. The more frequently a story was "shared" online, the more believable it seemed to be.

> "[Trump] wants to move to [. . .] a deeper level of relations with Russia. How can we not welcome that? Of course we welcome it."[11]

However, some of the people sharing those stories were people within the Trump campaign. For example, in November 2016, Mike Flynn, the man who served as Trump's national security adviser for only twenty-four days, tweeted a link to the PizzaGate story, implying that it was real and should be considered by voters. His son, Michael Flynn Jr., also tweeted about PizzaGate after the shooting, implying that the story was real because it had not yet been proven false.

President Trump himself has shared links and information about stories that have been proven false. For example, after assuming office, he infamously tweeted that President Obama had had his home, Trump Tower, wiretapped during the presidential campaign. Spying on American citizens is a civil rights violation, and

Michael Flynn

Michael Flynn is a former general and a business and political consultant. During 2016, he served as an effective surrogate for Donald Trump's presidential campaign, insisting that Trump was an outsider to politics who would be able to come to Washington and rid it of corruption.

When Trump won the presidential election, he appointed Flynn as his national security adviser. However, twenty-four days after his appointment, Flynn was forced to resign as part of a major controversy: it had been revealed that Flynn had held a telephone call with the Russian ambassador to the United States before Trump was inaugurated. During that call, Flynn discussed the current sanctions the United States was implementing against Russia. Later, when he reported the details of the call to Vice President Mike Pence, he did not mention that he discussed the sanctions. When it was revealed that he had discussed them, it was obvious that he'd lied to Pence—for that reason, he was forced to step down.

various intelligence agencies, including the FBI and the NSA, stated unequivocally that there was no evidence to indicate that Trump Tower had ever been wiretapped.

Both the US House of Representatives and the US Senate opened investigations into whether or not the Trump campaign had colluded with the Russians to throw the election in favor of Trump. During hearings before the House of Representatives investigating committee, FBI director James Comey stated that the FBI had also been investigating this very question since July 2016.

During the Senate hearings, in the spring of 2017, experts testified how "Russia's vast information warfare campaign, which involves at least 15,000 operatives worldwide writing and spreading false news stories and conspiracy theories online. [. . .] The campaign has targeted President Trump himself."[12] Former FBI agent Clinton Watts stated, "I can tell you right now, accounts tweet at President Trump during high volumes when they know he's online and they push conspiracy theories."[13] Watts added that President Trump has often repeated claims made originally in fake news stories pushed into the social media forum by the Russians.

Finally, business connections between Donald J. Trump and his staff and the Russians have been uncovered that may prove further evidence of collusion. For example, Secretary of State Rex Tillerson, a former CEO of Exxon, was given an award by Vladimir Putin— the Russian Order of Friendship—in 2013 for being a friendly partner of Russia. Also, Trump himself has sought financing from people close to Putin: "As major banks in America stopped lending him money following his many bankruptcies, the Trump organization was forced to seek financing from non-traditional institutions. Several had direct ties to Russian financial interests in ways that have raised eyebrows. What's more, several of Trump's senior advisors have business ties to Russia or its satellite politicians."[14]

The connection between Trump, his campaign, and Russia continues to be investigated at various levels

Russia and Syria

In 2011, a civil war broke out in the country of Syria. Its leader, President Bashar al-Assad, has been aligned closely with Vladimir Putin. Al-Assad has been heavily criticized for the inhumane way in which the Syrian military has attacked civilians and oppositional groups. However, Putin has stood steadily by the beleaguered Syrian leader, saying, "We will carry out air strikes and support Syrian army offensives for as long as the Syrian army carries them out."[15] The atrocities committed against the Syrian people have triggered a worldwide refugee crisis. On April 4, 2017, reports confirmed that al-Assad had ordered a chemical weapons attack on Syrians, killing over eighty people, including twenty-five children. It was the worst chemical attack in years. However, Putin continues to support al-Assad, perhaps as a way of regaining some leverage for Russia in the Middle East.

by several committees and organizations within the American government.

Russia in the World

Under Putin, Russia has undoubtedly regained some of its status as an important world power. However, Putin has been criticized for consolidating his own power and catering to the Russian oligarchs, a class of businessmen and businesswomen who have a tremendous amount of political influence.

In 2014, the Winter Olympics were held in Sochi, Russia, and it was a major moment for Russia—and for Putin. Billions were spent preparing the town for the international games, and the event was also meant to demonstrate to the world just how far Russia had advanced under Putin. However, before long, the games were immersed in scandal, as it was discovered that many of the Russian athletes had taken steroids.

In fact, an investigation found that, for years, a state-run program had been in effect, which administered steroids to over one thousand athletes in thirty different sports. Putin tried to cover up the issue: "We're against doping, above all because it is bad for human health. And those involved with doping should be punished."[16] However, the extent of the program, which was operated and managed by state officials, shocked the world, and many Russian athletes were banned from competing in the 2016 Olympics in Rio de Janeiro by the governing bodies of their individual sports. Once again, Putin had attempted to impress the world, but the effort resulted in more scandal and charges of corruption.

The 2014 Winter Olympics were held in Sochi, Russia. This was seen as a proud moment for Putin and the Russian people, until several Russian athletes were found to be illegally taking steroids.

What does Vladimir Putin's future hold? It is difficult to say. Despite the opinions of leaders in the West, who believe he has encouraged the erosion of democracy in Russia, it appears that he enjoys increasing popularity among his own people. A 2016 poll conducted by the Russian state revealed that an astounding 74 percent of

Russian voters would elect him to a fourth term.[17] Critics charge that that statistic is simply not based in fact.

Charges of corruption continue to dog Putin, but his ambitions run high. It remains to be seen if his personal involvement in interfering with national elections in the United States and other countries can be proven. One thing is clear: By creating confusion and chaos around the 2016 US presidential election, under Putin's leadership Russia has succeeded in an act of espionage against the world's foremost superpower that should not be underestimated.

Chronology

1952 Vladimir Putin is born in Leningrad (now St. Petersburg) on October 7, 1952.

1975 Putin graduates from Leningrad State University. Joins the KGB, the Soviet Union's security agency.

1983 Putin marries Lyudmila Shkrebneva.

1985 Putin is assigned to work for the KGB in East Germany. His first child, a daughter named Maria, is born.

1986 Putin's second daughter, Katerina, is born.

1990 Putin moves his family back to Leningrad, where he becomes active in local politics.

1991 Putin resigns from the KGB on August 20.

1994–1996 Putin becomes more active in local government in St. Petersburg.

1996 Putin is transferred to Moscow to work for President Boris Yeltsin in August.

1998 Putin is named head of the federal security service, the spy agency that succeeded the former KGB.

1999 Putin is appointed Russia's fifth prime minister in less than two years, in August, after a series of firings by an unstable Yeltsin. He becomes acting president on December 31, after Yeltsin's resignation.

2000 Putin is elected president of Russia on March 26. He asssumes office in May and pledges to work hard for the Russian people. On August 12, the submarine *Kursk* sinks in the Barents Sea, with a crew of 118 aboard. There are no survivors.

2001 Putin pledges to work with the United States and aid its efforts to fight terrorism after the attack on the World Trade Center and the Pentagon on September 11.

2002 Chechen militants seize the Dubrovka Theater in Moscow. Many Russian citizens die.

2004 Chechens take over a school in Beslan, which ends up in the deaths of hundreds of Russians, including many schoolchildren. Putin is re-elected to a second term as president.

2008 Putin is appointed prime minister by Russia's new president, Demitry Medvedev.

2011 Syrian civil war erupts. Putin is a staunch supporter of President al-Assad, despite the latter's many violations of human rights against his own citizens.

2012 Putin runs for president and is elected. Protests break out at his inauguration.

2013 Putin announces that he and Lyudmila are divorcing. He grants asylum to Edward Snowden, an American who leaked government secrets, in August.

2014 Russian athletes are implicated in steroid use, a doping scandal that soured Russia's hosting of the

Winer Olympics in Sochi. Russia annexes Crimea in March, causing an uproar over his destabilizing of Ukraine.

2016 Donald J. Trump is elected the forty-fifth president of the United States in November, which leads to suspicions that Russia, and especially Putin, interfered with the US election by hacking computers and spreading fake news on the internet.

2017 Scandal engulfs the new presidency of Donald J. Trump, as investigations are launched into whether or not his campaign colluded with Putin and the Russians during the election. Suspicions arise about Putin's hand in hacking of French presidential candidate Emmanuel Macron.

Chapter Notes

Introduction

1. Eliza Collins, "Poll: Clinton, Trump Most Unfavorable Candidates Ever," *USAToday*, August 31, 2016, http://www.usatoday.com/story/news/politics/onpolitics/2016/08/31/poll-clinton-trump-most-unfavorable-candidates-ever/89644296.

2. Robby Mook, "Russia's DNC Hack Was Only the Start," *New York Times*, January 10, 2017, https://www.nytimes.com/2017/01/10/opinion/russias-dnc-hack-was-only-the-start.html.

3. William M. Arkin, Ken Dilanian, and Cynthia McFadden, "U.S. Officials: Putin Personally Involved in U.S. Election Hack," NBC News, December 15, 2016, http://www.nbcnews.com/news/us-news/u-s-officials-putin-personally-involved-u-s-election-hack-n696146.

Chapter 1: A Challenging Childhood

1. Vladimir Putin, "An Ordinary Family," Vladimir Putin: Personal Website, http://en.putin.kremlin.ru/bio.

2. Joseph Burgo, "Vladimir Putin, Narcissist?" *Atlantic*, April 15, 2014, https://www.theatlantic.com/health/archive/2014/04/vladimir-putin-narcissist/360544.

3. "Seven Quotes That Reveal the Mind of Vladimir Putin," *Telegraph*, December 17, 2015, http://www.telegraph.co.uk/news/worldnews/europe/russia/12055826/Seven-quotes-that-show-Vladimir-Putin-is-still-in-charge.html.

4. Putin, "An Ordinary Family."

5. Burgo.

6. Vladimir Putin, "School Years," Vladimir Putin: Personal Website, http://en.putin.kremlin.ru/bio.

7. "Paper Reveals Putin's Cheeky Childhood," ABC News, March 14, 2017, http://abcnews.go.com/International/story?id=81394&page=1.

8. Putin, "School Years."

9. "Paper Reveals Putin's Cheeky Childhood."

10. Ibid.

11. Ibid.

12. Kavitha A. Davidson, "Vladimir Putin's Judo Skills Are Better Than Yours," *Huffington Post*, August 9, 2013, http://www.huffingtonpost.com/2013/08/08/vladimir-putin-judo_n_3726370.html.

13. Reiss Smith, "What Is the KGB? Vladimir Putin 'Set to Bring Back the Secret Soviet Spy Force,'" *Express*, September 28, 2016, http://www.express.co.uk/news/world/715391/what-is-the-kgb-russia-vladimir-putin-soviet-union-spy-force.

14. Ibid.

15. David Hoffman, "Putin's Career Rooted in Russia's KGB," *Washington Post*, January 30, 2000, http://www.washingtonpost.com/wp-srv/inatl/longterm/russiagov/putin.htm.

16. Chris Bowlby, "Vladimir Putin's Formative German Years," BBC, March 27, 2015, http://www.bbc.com/news/magazine-32066222.

Chapter 2: Personal Life

1. Vladimir Putin, "Wedding and Germany," Vladimir Putin: Personal Website, http://eng.putin.kremlin.ru/bio.

2. Ibid.

3. "Seven Quotes That Reveal the Mind of Vladimir Putin," *Telegraph*, December 17, 2015, http://www.telegraph.co.uk/news/worldnews/europe/russia/12055826/Seven-quotes-that-show-Vladimir-Putin-is-still-in-charge.html.

4. Chris Bowlby, "Vladimir Putin's Formative German Years," BBC, March 27, 2015, http://www.bbc.com/news/magazine-32066222.

5. Hasani Gittens, "Meet the Putins: Inside Russian Leader's Mysterious First Family," NBC News, July 26, 2014, http://www.nbcnews.com/news/world/meet-putins-inside-russian-leaders-mysterious-family-n164331.

6. Michael Kaplan, "A Rare, Tantalizing Peek into Putin's Secret Family Life," *New York Post*, December

26, 2015, http://nypost.com/2015/12/26/a-rare-peek-inside-vladimir-putins-family-secrets.

7. "Seven Quotes That Reveal the Mind of Vladimir Putin."

8. Serge Schmemann, "End of the Soviet Union," *New York Times*, December 26, 1991, http://www.nytimes.com/1991/12/26/world/end-of-the-soviet-union-the-soviet-state-born-of-a-dream-dies.html?pagewanted=all.

9. Ibid.

10. "Perestroika and Glasnost," History.com, 2010, http://www.history.com/topics/cold-war/perestroika-and-glasnost.

11. "End of the Soviet Union: Text of Gorbachev's Farewell Address," *New York Times*, December 26, 1991, http://www.nytimes.com/1991/12/26/world/end-of-the-soviet-union-text-of-gorbachev-s-farewell-address.html?pagewanted=all.

12. "Perestroika and Glasnost."

13. "The Gorbachev Visit; Excerpts From Speech to U.N. on Major Soviet Military Cuts," *New York Times*, December 8, 1988, http://www.nytimes.com/1988/12/08/world/the-gorbachev-visit-excerpts-from-speech-to-un-on-major-soviet-military-cuts.html?pagewanted=all.

Chapter 3: The Soviet Union in Crisis

1. Bridget Coaker, "Soviet Union Collapse in Picture," *Guardian*, July 14, 2014, https://www.theguardian.

com/world/gallery/2014/jul/14/soviet-union-collapse-in-pictures.

2. "Transcript: Putin's Prepared Remarks at 43rd Munich Conference on Security Policy," *Washington Post*, February 12, 2007, http://www.washingtonpost.com/wp-dyn/content/article/2007/02/12/AR2007021200555.html.

3. Jonathan Steele, "Mikhail Gorbachev: I Should Have Abandoned the Communist Party Earlier," *Guardian*, August 16, 2011, https://www.theguardian.com/world/2011/aug/16/gorbachev-guardian-interview.

4. Ibid.

5. Boris Yeltsin, "Yeltsin's Address to the Russian People" (speech, Moscow, August 19, 1991), Vancouver Island University, https://web.viu.ca/davies/H102/Yelstin.speech.1991.htm.

6. "End of the Soviet Union: Text of Gorbachev's Farewell Address," *New York Times*, December 26, 1991, http://www.nytimes.com/1991/12/26/world/end-of-the-soviet-union-text-of-gorbachev-s-farewell-address.html?pagewanted=all.

7. Robert V. Daniels, "From Gorbachev to Putin," *Nation*, October 1, 2008, https://www.thenation.com/article/gorbachev-putin.

8. Vladimir Putin, "Putin Address to the Nation: Excerpts," BBC, April 25, 2005, http://news.bbc.co.uk/2/hi/europe/4481455.stm.

9. Ibid.

10. Stepan Kravchenko, "Putin Says Soviet Union's Collapse Wasn't Inevitable," Bloomberg News, September 23, 2016, https://www.bloomberg.com/news/articles/2016-09-23/putin-says-soviet-union-s-collapse-wasn-t-inevitable.

11. "Russia's Yeltsin Known for Gaffes, Off-color Jokes," Reuters, April 23, 2007, http://www.reuters.com/article/us-russia-yeltsin-gaffes-idUSL2333853820070423.

12. Daniels.

Chapter 4: Putin's Rise to Politics

1. Steven Eke, "Yeltsin's Chechen Nightmare," BBC, April 24, 2007, http://news.bbc.co.uk/2/hi/europe/6588221.stm.

2. Ibid.

3. Michael Specter, "How the Chechen Guerrillas Shocked Their Russian Foes," *New York Times*, August 18, 1996, http://www.nytimes.com/1996/08/18/world/how-the-chechen-guerrillas-shocked-their-russian-foes.html?emc=eta1.

4. Robert V. Daniels, "From Gorbachev to Putin," *Nation*, October 1, 2008, https://www.thenation.com/article/gorbachev-putin.

5. Andrew Osborn, "Boris Yeltsin's Daughter Attacks Vladimir Putin," *Telegraph*, January 23, 2010, http://www.telegraph.co.uk/news/worldnews/

europe/7063201/Boris-Yeltsins-daughter-attacks-Vladimir-Putin.html.

6. "Yeltsin Redraws Political Map," BBC, August 10, 1999, http://news.bbc.co.uk/2/hi/europe/415087.stm.

7. Ibid.

8. Ibid.

9. "Transcript: Putin's Prepared Remarks at 43rd Munich Conference on Security Policy," *Washington Post*, February 12, 2007, http://www.washingtonpost.com/wp-dyn/content/article/2007/02/12/AR2007021200555.html.

10. "Yeltsin Linked to Bribe Scandal," BBC, September 8, 1999, http://news.bbc.co.uk/2/hi/business/441916.stm.

11. Andrew Foxall, "Chechnya, Russia's Forgotten War," *World Affairs Journal*, 2015, http://www.worldaffairsjournal.org/article/chechnya-russia%E2%80%99s-forgotten-war.

12. Ibid.

Chapter 5: President Putin

1. "Vladimir Putin: Spy Turned Politician," BBC, January 1, 2000, http://news.bbc.co.uk/2/hi/europe/415124.stm.

2. Robert V. Daniels, "From Gorbachev to Putin," *Nation*, October 1, 2008, https://www.thenation.com/article/gorbachev-putin.

3. Michael McFaul, "Testimony: Russia's 2000 Presidential Elections," Carnegie Endowment for International Peace, April 1, 2000, http://carnegieendowment.org/2000/04/01/russia-s-2000-presidential-elections-implications-for-russian-democracy-and-u.s.-russian-relations-pub-421.

4. "Putin's Inauguration Speech," BBC, May 7, 2000, http://news.bbc.co.uk/2/hi/world/monitoring/media_reports/739432.stm.

5. McFaul.

6. Ibid.

7. "Putin's Inauguration Speech."

8. Marcus Warren, "Putin Faces the Fury of the Kursk Widows," Telegraph, August 23, 2000, http://www.telegraph.co.uk/news/worldnews/europe/russia/1367319/Putin-faces-fury-of-the-Kursk-widows.html.

9. Douglas Waller, "Putin Gets a Win on US Missile Defense Plan," *Time,* September 1, 2000, http://content.time.com/time/nation/article/0,8599,53909,00.html.

10. Ibid.

11. Pete Baumgartner, "Bill Clinton in 2000: Putin 'Could Get Squishy on Democracy,'" Radio Liberty, January 8, 2016, http://www.rferl.org/a/bill-clinton-putin-could-get-squishy-on-democracy/27477287.html.

12. Warren.

13. "What Really Happened to Russia's 'Unsinkable' Sub," *Guardian*, August 4, 2001, https://www. theguardian.com/world/2001/aug/05/kursk.russia.

14. Ben Aris, "Doomed Sailor's Letter from the Kursk," *Telegraph*, October 27, 2000, http://www.telegraph. co.uk/news/worldnews/europe/norway/1372059/ Doomed-sailors-letter-from-the-Kursk.html.

15. Warren.

16. Ibid.

Chapter 6: Putin Invades the Crimea

1. Alec Luhn, "15 Ways of Vladimir Putin," *Guardian*, May 6, 2015, https://www.theguardian.com/ world/2015/may/06/vladimir-putin-15-ways-he- changed-russia-world.

2. Albert Oetgen and Tom Balmforth, "The Dubrovka Theater Siege in Moscow, a Decade Later," *Atlantic*, October 23, 2012, https://www.theatlantic.com/ international/archive/2012/10/the-dubrovka- theater-siege-in-moscow-a-decade-later/263931.

3. William Schneider, "Ukraine's Orange Revolution," *Atlantic*, December 2004, https://www.theatlantic. com/magazine/archive/2004/12/ukraines-orange- revolution/305157.

4. Adrian Karatnycky, "Ukraine's Orange Revolution," *Foreign Affairs*, March/April 2005, https://www. foreignaffairs.com/articles/russia-fsu/2005-03-01/ ukraines-orange-revolution.

5. Victor Yushchenko, "Independence Day Speech," *Ukrainian Weekly*, September 4, 2005, http://www. ukrweekly.com/old/archive/2005/360523.shtml.

6. David Randall, "Yushchenko Was Poisoned by Soup Laced with Dioxin," *Independent*, December 12, 2004, http://www.independent.co.uk/news/world/ europe/yushchenko-was-poisoned-by-soup-laced- with-dioxin-684338.html.

7. Kim Sengupta, "Viktor Yushchenko: 'Every Politician in Ukraine Who Turns to the West Is in Danger,'" *Independent*, October 14, 2015, http:// www.independent.co.uk/news/people/viktor- yushchenko-every-politician-in-ukraine-who- turns-to-the-west-is-in-danger-a6694311.html.

8. "Ukraine Suspends Preparations for EU Trade Agreement," BBC, November 21, 2013, http://www. bbc.com/news/world-europe-25032275.

9. "Transcript: Vladimir Putin's April 17th Q&A," *Washington Post*, April 17, 2014, https://www. washingtonpost.com/world/transcript-vladimir- putins-april-17-qanda/2014/04/17/ff77b4a2- c635-11e3-8b9a-8e0977a24aeb_story.html?utm_ term=.1260a9257d4a.

10. "Ukrainian Crisis: Timeline," BBC News, November 13, 2014, http://www.bbc.com/news/ world-middle-east-26248275.

11. Caroline Mortimer, "Ukraine Crisis," *Independent*, March 3, 2014, http://www.independent.co.uk/

news/world/europe/ukraine-crisis-why-is-crimea-so-important-to-russia-9166447.html.

12. "Transcript: Vladimir Putin's April 17th Q&A."

13. Vladimir Putin, "Address by President of the Russian Federation," March 18, 2014, http://en.kremlin.ru/events/president/news/20603.

14. "Joint Statement on Crimea," March 18, 2014, https://www.consilium.europa.eu/uedocs/cms_data/docs/pressdata/en/ec/141628.pdf.

Chapter 7: US Elections

1. Joby Warrick and Karen DeYoung, "From Reset to Pause: The Real Story Behind Hillary Clinton's Feud with Vladimir Putin," *Washington Post*, November 3, 2016, https://www.washingtonpost.com/world/national-security/from-reset-to-pause-the-real-story-behind-hillary-clintons-feud-with-vladimir-putin/2016/11/03/f575f9fa-a116-11e6-8832-23a007c77bb4_story.html?utm_term=.519d9c5a1be8.

2. Ibid.

3. Ibid.

4. Alana Abramson and Shushannah Walshe, "The 4 Most Damaging Emails from the DNC WikiLeaks Dump," ABC News, July 25, 2016, http://abcnews.go.com/Politics/damaging-emails-dnc-wikileaks-dump/story?id=40852448.

5. Jeff Pegues, "U.S. Intelligence Believes DNC Email Hack Ordered by Putin," CBS News, December

15, 2016, http://www.cbsnews.com/news/us-intelligence-believes-dnc-email-hack-ordered-by-russian-president-vladimir-putin.

6. Andrew Roth and Dana Priest, "Putin Wants Revenge and Respect, and Hacking the US Is His Way of Getting It," *Washington Post*, September 16, 2016, https://www.washingtonpost.com/world/europe/russian-hacking-a-question-of-revenge-and-respect/2016/09/15/8bcc8d7e-7511-11e6-9781-49e591781754_story.html?tid=a_inl&utm_term=.452e970c0633.

7. "Seven Quotes That Reveal the Mind of Vladimir Putin," *Telegraph*, December 17, 2015, http://www.telegraph.co.uk/news/worldnews/europe/russia/12055826/Seven-quotes-that-show-Vladimir-Putin-is-still-in-charge.html.

8. Bryan Schatz, "A History of Donald Trump's Bromance with Vladimir Putin," *Mother Jones*, October 5, 2016. http://www.motherjones.com/politics/2016/10/trump-putin-timeline

9. Ibid.

10. Ibid.

11. Jeff Nesbit, "Donald Trump's Many, Many, Many, Many Ties to Russia," *Time*, August 15, 2016, http://time.com/4433880/donald-trump-ties-to-russia.

12. Jeff Pegues, "'Follow the Trail of Dead Russians': Senate Hears Testimony on 'Cyber Invasion,'" CBS News, March 30, 2017, http://www.cbsnews.com/news/russian-meddling-investigation-

misinformation-tactics-senate-intelligence-committee.

13. Ibid.

14. Nesbit.

15. Shaun Walker, "Putin Admits Russian Military Presence in Ukraine for First Time," *Guardian*, December 17, 2015, https://www.theguardian.com/world/2015/dec/17/vladimir-putin-admits-russian-military-presence-ukraine.

16. "Seven Quotes That Reveal the Mind of Vladimir Putin."

17. Damien Sharkov, "Majority of Russian Voters Back Putin for Fourth Term: Poll," *Newsweek*, March 3, 2016, http://www.newsweek.com/putin-backed-74-percent-majority-voters-fourth-term-poll-433003.

Glossary

annexation A process by which one nation incorporates another nation into its borders.

Communism An economic system that emerged from the theory of socialism.

Communist Party The ruling party of the former Soviet Union.

coup d'état The overthrow of a government.

democratic centralism A political ideal of Vladimir Lenin's that was a compromise between democracy and pragmatic efficiency.

Federal Security Service The renamed and restructured KGB.

glasnost Soviet policy, instituted by Mikhail Gorbachev, of openness to political and social debate and discussion.

KGB Acronym for the Komitet Gosudarstvennoy Bezopasnosti, the security and intelligence agency of the former Soviet Union.

kommunalka Post-war Soviet communal residence building.

Orange Revolution A political, pro-democratic revolution that took place in Ukraine between November and December 2004.

perestroika The political movement led by Mikhail Gorbachev for a restructuring of the authoritarian government.

politburo One of the authoritarian bodies of the government of the former Soviet Union.

president The head of all three branches of the Russian government.

prime minister The head of the executive branch of the Russian government.

Russia An ethnically diverse nation that is the largest country in the world; currently, it is led by President Vladimir Putin.

Soviet Union An empire, which embraced Communism, that was a world superpower between 1917 and 1991.

Further Reading

Books

Gessen, Masha. *The Man Without a Face: The Unlikely Rise of Vladimir Putin*. New York, NY: Riverhead Books, 2015.

Kasparov, Garry. *Winter Is Coming: Why Vladimir Putin and the Enemies of the Free World Must Be Stopped*. New York, NY: Public Affairs, 2016.

Meyers, Steven Lee. *The New Tsar: The Rise and Reign of Vladimir Putin*. New York, NY: Vintage, 2016.

Nance, Malcolm. *The Plot to Hack America: How Putin's Cyberspies and WikiLeaks Tried to Steal the 2016 Election*. New York, NY: Skyhorse Publishing, 2016.

Websites

History–Putin

http://www.history.com/topics/vladimir-putin
A summary of Putin and his life.

Vladimir Putin

http://www.biography.com/people/vladimir-putin-9448807
A biography of the Russian president.

Vladimir Putin

http://eng.putin.kremlin.ru/bio
The official Kremlin website for Putin.

Films

Putin's Way. PBS. Frontline documentary. January 13, 2015. http://www.pbs.org/wgbh/frontline/film/putins-way.

The Most Powerful Man in the World. CNN. March 2017.

Index